Naked Guide to
BONDS

Naked Guide to
BONDS
What You Need to Know—
Stripped Down
to the Bare Essentials

Michael V. Brandes

WILEY

John Wiley & Sons, Inc.

Published by John Wiley & Sons, Inc., Hoboken, New Jersey.

Published simultaneously in Canada.

For general information on our other products and services, or technical support, please contact our Customer Care Department within the United States at 800-762-2974, outside the United States at 317-572-3993 or fax 317-572-4002.

Wiley also publishes its books in a variety of electronic formats. Some content that appears in print may not be available in electronic books.

For more information about Wiley products, visit our web site at www.wiley.com.

ISBN 0-471-46221-7

Printed in the United States of America

10 9 8 7 6 5 4 3 2 1

To Nadine Reilly,
whose fortitude and compassion
surpassed my comprehension long ago.

And to my Mother, Elizabeth Vilella Brandes,
who always gave me one word of advice.

CONTENTS

PREFACE

As any successful investor knows—the *real* secret to success is that *there are no secrets*. And despite your neighbor's claims to the contrary, there are no shortcuts either. There are, however, some ways to learn about investing that are more palatable than others. That's why this book was written.

In fact, I like to think of *Naked Guide to Bonds* as an anti-textbook—lean and easy to read. It's a simple—but not simplistic—primer written for investors who want to nail down the essentials about the bond market in a time-efficient manner. I call it the *Naked Guide*™ approach, and it's designed for those of us who barely find time to do the things we want to do—let alone the stuff that's important.

Of course, for some of you, no investment book could be short enough—even one that professes to cut out all the fat. That's OK, because summary points are provided at the beginning of each chapter. So if you decide to skip it, well, at least you'll have a general idea of what you're missing. You'll also notice that each chapter gradually builds upon the information that precedes it. That way, you won't be overwhelmed by anything right from the beginning, or be thrown for a loop.

Although research is my profession, education also describes what I do. This book provides answers to many of the questions I get every day. And it's written in a manner that's been shaped by an especially familiar refrain: *just tell me what I need to know*. Well, here it is. Because, when you come right down to it, you don't need to be a Wall Street analyst or a finance professor to be a smart and successful bond investor.

Michael Brandes
Greenwich Village, New York City

ACKNOWLEDGMENTS

First, I'd like to thank Kathleen McNamara, who generously provided invaluable feedback and insightful criticisms; Michael Venezia and Timothy Baker, who were tireless sounding boards as the book progressed; James Donofrio, Michael Baumeister, Keith Knoop, and Kris Xippolitos for their thoughtful comments and market expertise; James Vlogianitis, Jane Vigna, and Lisa Correia for sharing their extensive trading knowledge; and Tom Anguilla, David Glick, Jonathan Mackay, Mike Kafantaris, J.P. Connellan, Vincent Esposito, Keith Douglas, Megan Messina and Jennifer Nicoletti for providing important insights on their respective disciplines. Gratitude is also due Stan Carnes, Lisa Finstrom, Lakhbir Hayre, Louise Yamada, and Mark Walker for their support.

Thanks to Bill Falloon, my editor, who gave me the opportunity and coaxed this project to fruition; Melissa Scuereb for her patience and diligence; Joanna Pomeranz and her team at PV&M for their production expertise; Denise Howard for her hard work and talented execution of the exhibits featured in this book; Derek Hodel for his friendship and professional guidance; and to Miss Kittles, who first encouraged me to write.

Last, but not least, I'd like to thank my family and friends for their infinite understanding and support during the writing of this book—especially for putting up with my hermit-like existence. Special thanks to my mother, who never stopped posting my stuff on the refrigerator; Karen and Peter Kruszon, for their unwavering generosity and encouragement; Mark, Casey, Emily, and Ryan, who will be forced to read this book one day; and to David and Cecilia Brandes for their patience and support. And finally, a debt of gratitude to Nadine Reilly, whose intellect and candor were indispensable.

Make your money in stocks. Keep your money in bonds.

Old investment adage

I wrote long because I didn't have time to write short.

Old writer's adage

PART ONE
What You Want to Know

chapter one
WHY BONDS?

The Bare Essentials

- A balanced portfolio of stocks and bonds can help most investors accomplish long-term investment goals more effectively than a pure equity strategy.
- Bonds provide solutions for two of the three most basic investment requirements: *income* and *capital preservation*.
- A bond is a security that pays a specified rate of interest for a limited amount of time and returns principal on a defined date.

Despite the diversity and breadth of today's media, the stock market inevitably dominates business news. You'd think there was nothing else to talk about. To be sure, the bond market occasionally takes center stage—usually when the Federal Reserve is about to make an announcement or when inflation concerns suddenly begin to percolate—but for the most part that's the exception, not the rule.

Of course, the motivations of news editors are easy to decipher. Much like homicides and natural disasters, the stock market simply generates better headlines than the sleepy bond market. I guess it's because all the elements of suspense are there, with quick fortunes made (and lost) more often in stocks than in bonds. Frankly, I'd be hard pressed to disagree—stocks *are* more newsworthy than bonds. So I'm not going to waste your time arguing to the contrary. But consider this: after the dramatic stock market decline that began in 2000, bonds outperformed equities for three years in a row. Now *that's* newsworthy.

I would also contend that a balanced portfolio of stocks and bonds can help most of you accomplish long-term investment goals more effectively than a pure equity strategy. This is not an original idea. With rare exception, stocks and bonds represent the two largest components of the three main asset classes recommended by most investment firms (the other would be cash). Consequently, the question is not whether you should own stocks *or* bonds, but how much of your investment portfolio should be allocated to each asset class.

You see, bonds provide solutions for two of the three most basic investment requirements: *Income* and *capital preservation*. The other objective, *growth,* is more appropriately achieved through stock investing. That's why stocks and bonds complement each other so well. Together, your bases are covered.

But we're getting a little ahead of ourselves here. Now that you understand some of the most compelling reasons why bonds are important, let's take a step back and briefly discuss what they are. Ironically, the best way to do this is to forget about bonds for a moment and instead think about what happens when you purchase a home. A loan officer informs you that the bank would be happy to lend you money as long as you promise to repay it in 15 or 30 years. Suppose you settle on a 30-year term. That's fine, but there's one more important caveat—it'll cost you, say, 6.75 percent annual interest for the privilege. It seems fair, so you sign the loan agreement.

It's the same scenario when you purchase a bond, except *you're the bank,* so *you're making the loan*. And as the bank, you expect borrowers to repay loans by a specific date and at an agreed-upon rate of interest. That's how bonds work. In other words, as a bondholder, your purchase is effectively a loan that will be repaid after a certain length of time and, during the life of the loan, you'll be paid a fixed rate of interest. That's why bonds are also known as *fixed-income securities*.

chapter two

WHO ISSUES BONDS? AND WHY?

The Bare Essentials

- Investment banks are hired to structure bond offerings, advise issuers on the timing and terms of sale, and arrange distribution to investors.

- Bond issuers are required to publish a *prospectus*—a document that outlines the key provisions of each offering.

- The public sector comprises federal government issues, known as *Treasuries,* and state and local government issues, known as *municipals.* Bond proceeds fill financing gaps and help smooth out the receipt of tax revenue.

- The private sector comprises corporations that issue bonds as an alternative to bank loans and stock offerings. Bond offerings provide companies with an efficient way to raise capital and does not dilute shareholder equity.

The bond market does not discriminate like the stock market—call it an equal opportunity marketplace. That's because it provides financing for *both* the private and public sectors. In fact, nearly every government and most major corporations in the world issue bonds—from the nations of

Great Britain and Brazil, to familiar household names such as IBM, Ford and Nestlé.

Here's a little known factoid that's guaranteed to amaze your family and friends: according to the Bond Market Association, the size of the U.S. bond market approached *$21 trillion* by the middle of 2003. That's more than the market capitalization of the New York Stock Exchange, American Stock Exchange, and NASDAQ listed companies *combined*. It's simply the largest securities market in the world.

It all starts with an issuer who contacts an investment bank to arrange—or *underwrite*—a bond sale. The bank (now considered the *underwriter*) advises the issuer on the timing and terms of the offering, such as the amount of bonds to issue and the interest rate. The underwriter also organizes a group of other investment firms, known as a *syndicate*, to help market the new bonds to prospective buyers, like you. The new securities also are sold to institutions, such as insurance companies and pension funds (see Figure 2.1). And just like each of us is assigned a nine-digit Social Security number, every bond is assigned a nine-digit (alphanumeric) CUSIP (Committee on Uniform Securities Identification Procedures) number.

When the deal is structured, the syndicate presents the terms to their clients who, in turn, submit *indications of interest*. The interest rate that's been proffered is usually adjusted to accommodate investor demand and to reflect prevailing market conditions. Issuers appoint banks as *trustees* to administer interest payments. Finally, the new bond is issued in the *primary market*, much like an initial public offering (IPO) for a stock. Subsequently, the bond would trade in the *secondary market*, where all previously-issued, or *outstanding*, securities are bought and sold.

Whenever a bond is created, issuers are required to publish a formal agreement that comprehensively describes the specific terms and conditions of the offering. This legally binding contract, known as an *inden-*

Issuer ⟶ Investment bank ⟶ Investment bank organizes syndicate ⟶ Investors

FIGURE 2.1   Creating a Bond

ture, contains provisions meant to protect both parties. *Covenants* spell out the legal protections provided to investors.

Although the indenture includes important information about a bond issue, it's also a complicated document that's been designed as a cure for insomnia. Consequently, its appeal is largely limited to masochistic investors who can't get enough of the fine print.

Crucial information from the indenture is summarized in an eminently more readable document known as the *prospectus*—an appropriate name because it's distributed to prospective buyers whenever a new security is offered. It clearly outlines the key provisions of an offering, including the use of proceeds, a description of the issuer, and risk factors to consider.

Investment firms are required to provide a prospectus to any client interested in a bond offering. Subsequent to issuance, however, you'll have a harder time finding a printed copy. Fortunately, the U.S. Securities and Exchange Commission (SEC) provides investors with online access to publicly filed offering documents at *www.sec.gov*. Although many experienced bond investors have never laid eyes on a prospectus, you'd be well-advised to review it before making a purchase. It may require a few extra cups of coffee to thoroughly review, but you'll be rewarded with a complete understanding of the offering.

Although nearly all bond issuers participate in this process, the most important player in the bond market—the federal government—does not. We'll discuss how these bonds reach investors in Chapter 15 when we discuss Treasury securities.

Public Sector

The public sector comprises federal, state, and local municipalities. It is dominated by two types of securities—federally issued bonds known as *Treasuries*, and state and local issues known as *municipals*.

Tax revenue and fees provide governments and their agencies with funding used for ongoing expenditures. These include income taxes, sales taxes, and any revenue-generating projects, such as tolls from roads and bridges. Problem is, governments don't collect enough from the likes of you and me to cover the large budget expenditures needed for public services.

That's where bonds come in. Besides filling financing gaps, they provide a way to smooth out government tax receipts, especially since tax revenue tends to fluctuate with changing economic conditions, can be seasonal, and is received over time. The alternative, of course, would be to raise taxes. And how many elected politicians today would prefer that course of action?

Bond issuance is especially important when large capital infusions are necessary, say, to build a new school or library. It enables governments to quickly raise a significant amount of money without placing undue strain on limited financial resources. For example, let's say state income taxes have steadily declined as unemployment has risen. The state might issue bonds to close the widening shortfall between tax revenue and money needed for public expenditures. Or how about the federal budget? In the 2002 fiscal year, the federal budget surplus became a deficit due to tax breaks and increased spending that coincided with an extended economic slowdown. This caused revenues to plummet, which has accelerated the pace of federal government bond issuance.

Private Sector

The private sector consists of domestic and multinational corporations. These companies issue bonds to satisfy a wide range of financial needs—from making acquisitions to building new factories. Essentially, bonds provide an alternative to stock issuance and bank loans.

The bond market also provides the private sector with an efficient way to raise funds—billions of dollars can be borrowed from thousands of investors in one day. Of course, publicly traded corporations could just issue more common stock, but there are compelling reasons to issue bonds instead. First of all, interest paid to bondholders provides a pretax deduction—known as *interest expense*—to corporations. This is similar to the tax break you receive when mortgage interest is deducted from your annual income—it lowers your overall tax bill.

Another reason corporations issue bonds rather than stock is because it's less likely to conflict with shareholder interests. When companies increase stock issuance, it reduces the percentage of the company that is owned by current shareholders. In other words, same size pie, more slices. That's called *diluting shareholder equity*. Additionally, the law of supply and demand suggests that if demand remains unchanged, more issuance could cause prices to decline.

Stock issuance, however, has some real advantages. Most importantly, proceeds from a stock sale never have to be repaid since investors receive partial ownership in the corporation. Additionally, stock dividends are *optional*. That means they could be suspended if a company were struggling or if its board of directors deemed profits could be more productively used elsewhere.

Interest payments on bonds, by the way, *are not optional*. In fact, corporate issuers must continue to pay bondholders for the life of the loan unless they're ready to declare bankruptcy. Then the bonds are considered *in default*. This rule applies to public sector bonds as well—*pay up, or go bankrupt*.

A record number of companies faced this dilemma during the economic downturn that greeted the new millennium. They simply borrowed too much and—when the music stopped—they didn't have enough money to continue servicing their debt. Sort of like running up the balance on your credit cards and then losing your job—at the very least you'd have to continue with minimum monthly payments. If you couldn't meet these or other debt obligations, you could be faced with personal bankruptcy.

The bond market is equally ruthless with issuers. Because it doesn't matter whether those securities were issued for some well-intentioned public purpose, were part of a smart tax-advantaged corporate strategy, or were preferable to diluting shareholder equity—all bondholders must receive regular interest payments. No excuses permitted. These standards don't provide much wiggle room for issuers, but they provide great comfort for bond investors.

chapter three
HOW ARE BONDS BOUGHT AND SOLD?

The Bare Essentials

🍂 Most bonds are bought and sold over the phone through a *broker-dealer*.

🍂 Unlike stocks, bonds are largely transacted over-the-counter and are not listed on a centralized exchange.

🍂 Although the Internet currently provides many advantages, investors should be wary of purchasing bonds online.

Most bonds are bought and sold the old-fashioned way: by agreeing to a transaction over the phone with a broker. Brokers work at investment firms that broker (sell) and deal (issue) bonds—hence the name broker-dealer. These broker-dealers are typically large firms that maintain substantial bond inventories, such as Smith Barney, Merrill Lynch, and Morgan Stanley.

Despite the growth of alternative distribution channels, the dominance of large broker-dealers has not waned. The explanation for this is as obvious as the reason that people rob banks—that's where the money is. When it comes to large broker-dealers, well, that's where the bonds are.

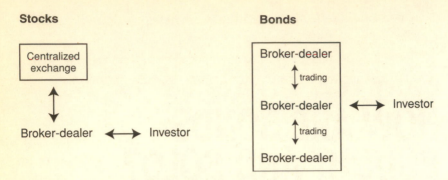

FIGURE 3.1   Buying and Selling Stocks and Bonds

The bulk of the bond market's huge daily trading volume is transacted in the virtual *over-the-counter* (*OTC*) market. *Virtual* means that it doesn't exist in any one place. In other words, unlike stocks, bond traders buy and sell directly with each other, not through a specialist on an organized exchange (see Figure 3.1).

Since most bonds are neither monitored nor tracked by an exchange, other than calling a broker, where do you look to find current bond prices? The simple answer is—it's complicated. Although prices of some securities are featured in newspapers and on financial web sites, that's the exception in the bond market, not the rule. What about the prices that are listed? Well, they can often be for institutional-size trades of at least $1 million or more—levels that usually do not apply to individual investors. That's because the bond market is largely dominated by institutional participants.

To be sure, there are nearly 400 bonds listed on the American Stock Exchange and over 2,000 on the New York Stock Exchange (NYSE) which, by the way, prides itself as being the "largest centralized bond market of any U.S. exchange." (It's true!) But even though there are a few well-traded issuers on the Big Board, such as AT&T, most NYSE–listed bonds are likely to trade OTC. That is, unless you own fewer than 10 bonds. In this case, your order would be subject to the *9 bond rule,* which requires customer orders of fewer than 10 listed bonds to be sent to the exchange floor. Nevertheless, since most bonds are not on the exchange, prices reflected there usually are not good indications of current market value.

Efforts are now underway to create more *price transparency* in the bond market, in other words, to monitor bond transactions like stocks with a system that compels broker-dealers to report each of their trades. The Bond Market Association, which represents a diverse mix of over 100 investment firms and banks, is at the forefront of these efforts and has made real progress in some areas, particularly in the municipal bond arena. For instance, you could view trade details reported daily on their web site (*www.investinginbonds.com*). Even though prices are from the previous business day, they give you a good sense of current market value. It's a free service, and it's recently been expanded to include some corporate bonds as well.

Transacting Online?

Speaking of web sites, the Internet undoubtedly has empowered investors in many ways. After all, real-time market information and the latest news are instantly available at the click of a mouse. You even can view your holdings online. But unless you're purchasing U.S. government securities or mutual funds, the promise of buying and selling most bonds on the Internet is just that—*a promise*.

I know that might be hard to believe, especially given the affordability and ease of online stock trading and the growing availability of bond offerings online. However, there's an important caveat to purchasing bonds on the Internet—most online brokers and discount firms do not maintain their own inventory. Surprised? After all, wouldn't you naturally assume that bonds shown on a web site would be owned by that dealer? In fact, most online offerings are from the same "inventory" provided by such companies as ValuBond, which essentially provide turnkey "dealer platforms" for brokers.

Why is this important to know? Because investment firms that don't maintain their own inventory have to purchase and sell bonds through other broker-dealers, transaction costs tend to rise each time a new layer is added. Don't get me wrong—I'm not implying that all online venues are not competitive. But just be wary of lower commission and rapid execution promises and make sure you shop around before investing online.

To be sure, some large broker-dealers feature direct online access to their bond inventory. And there's no question that institutional business has become especially well developed. In fact, due to an enormous investment in technology, electronic trading platforms now enable broker-dealers to transact directly with each other and with their institutional clients.

Increased institutional market activity has enhanced price transparency, which in turn has facilitated more competition. These developments should benefit individual investors since, after all, more competition usually produces lower prices. However, the benefits of online bond trading cannot be compared with the ease and convenience of purchasing stocks online. So even though we'll be talking about online resources throughout this book, I'm going to put myself out on a limb and skip the standard chapter that pays homage to the Internet. Just in case you go looking for it.

chapter four

WHY BUY BONDS RATHER THAN STOCKS?

The Bare Essentials

- Bonds provide investors with an effective way to preserve capital and generate income.
- Stocks are more appropriate for growth objectives.

Stocks and bonds are essentially two sides of the same coin—the former bestow ownership representing equity, while the latter confer creditorship (OK, I made that word up) representing debt. That's why their markets are known as the *equity* and *debt* markets, respectively. It's the reason we hear stocks and bonds often uttered in the same breath—they have complementary characteristics. As an Eastern philosopher-turned-investor might observe, it's the market's very own yin and yang.

Just as there are a number of pros and cons related to the issuance of stocks and bonds, there are a number of pros and cons related to an investment in either of these securities. First and foremost, there's a distinct difference in growth potential. After all, everyone knows that stock—not bond—prices could go to the moon. But—as many of us have been harshly reminded—stocks also retain the destructive capacity to crash down to earth. Remember when Internet darling Yahoo! traded above $200? How about Lucent—AT&T's former brain trust—when its stock traded over $60? Both of these stocks declined more than 90% within 18 months of hitting their respective highs.

When you come right down to it, the only downside protection provided by a stock is that it cannot trade below zero. For that reason, the stock market is just not the place to invest most of your money if your primary objective is *capital preservation.* After all, only bonds promise to return your principal on a specific date. Of course, it's a trade-off (what isn't?) since you'll be giving up the growth potential typically associated with equities. And, just like stocks, bond prices fluctuate. But if you're a buy-and-hold investor who purchases high-quality securities, you can rest assured that principal risk is minimized.

Bonds also provide investors with dependable income streams, which is why they're popular with retired investors. Of course, you could just buy a dividend-paying stock, but good luck finding one that pays a decent dividend. The average dividend paid by an S&P 500 company (the 500 largest publicly traded companies by market capitalization) is currently less than 2.0 percent. That means if you're attempting to supplement retirement income, it's going to take a whole lot of stock to really make a difference to your bottom line.

It wasn't always that way. Some issuers—particularly telephone and electric utility companies—used to pay relatively high dividends. However, these monopolies were dismantled as widespread government deregulation gained momentum in the 1980s. Additionally, investors started to focus on stock price appreciation, and executive compensation became tied to equity performance. As a result, corporate priorities shifted from increasing dividends to boosting the company's stock price.

Bond investors may instead replace these low dividends with predictable interest payments. The operative word there is "predictable" because, even if changes to the U.S. tax code begin to boost dividends, it still doesn't alter the fact that stock dividends are optional. That means a company's board of directors has the discretion to increase, decrease, or even eliminate the dividend at any time. As we discussed in the last chapter, no such discretion exists over the interest income generated by bonds.

Don't get me wrong; I'm not suggesting that it's time to liquidate your stock portfolio. After all, a rising stock is going to provide you with the kind of price appreciation that simply cannot be matched by bonds. However, the complementary strengths of the bond market could help you more effectively offset equity market risks and balance your overall financial objectives. We'll talk more about this later when we discuss the importance of diversification.

PART TWO
Essential Parts

chapter five
PRICE

The Bare Essentials

- Bonds have a *bid* price and an *offer* (also called *ask*) price. You sell a bond at the bid and buy a bond at the offer. The bid is always lower than the offer, and the difference is called the *bid/offer spread*.

- When a bond's price trades above its $1,000 par value, it is said to be trading at a *premium*. When it trades below par, it is said to be trading at a *discount*.

- Bonds are typically quoted as a percentage of par value, rather than in dollars. For example, $1,020 would simply be 102.

- Bonds trade with accrued interest, which is the amount of interest accumulated, but not paid, between semiannual payment dates.

Bond prices rise and fall for a multitude of reasons. We'll review these in the next section, but—if you simply can't stand the suspense—let's just say it's largely due to interest rate fluctuations.

All bonds have two price levels, or *quotes*, known as the *bid* and the *offer* (also called the *ask*). Traders purchase (or bid) for bonds at the bid price and sell them at the offer price. (The next time you're sauntering past a trading desk, yell over to a trader and say, "Hey, Buddy. Gimme a bid for that bond." They love that.) Since no trader is going to sell a bond below cost, the bid will always be lower than the offer. Makes sense, right? So when you sell a bond, you'll receive the bid price (known as "hitting the bid"), and when you purchase a bond, you'll pay the offer price. These two prices often appear together. When they do, the bid always appears first and the offer appears second. For example, if a bond is bid at $990 and is offered at $1,010, the bid/offer is $990/$1,010.

The difference between the bid and offer is called the *bid/offer spread*. In the previous example, it would be $20. The size of the spread is not fixed, and it'll inevitably change according to the type of security and prevailing market conditions. The trader profits from the spread, which in other businesses is called the *margin*.

Bonds are commonly issued in multiples of $1,000, also known as *par value*, or *face value*. For instance, if your portfolio includes 100 bonds, the total par value would be $100,000 (100 bonds × $1,000 par). When a bond trades equal to its par value, it's said to be trading *at par*. However, since market prices are not static, bonds seldom trade exactly at par. Instead, they regularly trade above par, at a *premium*, or below par, at a *discount* (see Figure 5.1). Under stable market conditions, bond prices typically range within 10% of their $1000 par value. However, a variety of factors cause some to trade in a much wider range, but we'll talk more about that later.

Bond prices usually are quoted as a percentage of par value rather than in dollars. This shorthand is actually pretty straightforward—you

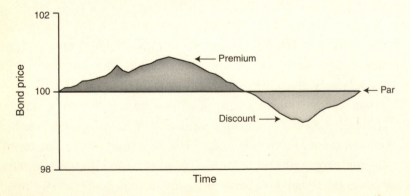

FIGURE 5.1 Par, Premium, and Discount

just move the decimal point one place to the left. For example, a $1,000 par bond is quoted as 100. A $1,020 premium bond is 102, and a $990 discount bond is simply 99. Conversely, if the bid/offer is quoted at 99/100, you just add a zero (or multiply it by 10) and it magically transforms back into its dollar price: $990/$1,000. What's the bid/offer spread? That's right, $10, or 1 point.

Let's take it a step further—suppose you want to buy 50 bonds quoted at 99/100. What's the total purchase price? Since each bond costs 100, or $1,000, you multiply that by 50 and get $50,000. Remember, though, to sell those 50 bonds, use the bid instead. Then your proceeds would be $990 × 50 = $49,500.

Got it? Good, because it gets a little more complicated. You see—just like the real world—bond prices are seldom neat, with nice round numbers. Think about it—how often does the total cost of any purchase fall exactly on the dollar? That is, without any cents? Well, you should expect the same result in the fixed-income market, namely because bond prices trade in 32nds. But don't worry, it's not as bad as it sounds.

We just learned that bond prices are commonly expressed as a percentage of par value, not in dollars. Well, the value of each one of those percentage points is further divided into 32 parts. That's it. Pretty painless, right? In practice, bonds are often quoted in eighths (4/32nds), which equals 0.125 (4 ÷ 32).

Let's say 50 bonds are offered at 99¾. Just multiply 99.75 by 50 to determine how much you'll pay for each bond—in this case, $997.50. Then multiply that by 50 to determine the total principal you'll owe ($997.50 × 50 = $49,875).

The price may instead be listed as 99.24, 99-24, or 99:24 (as in 24/32nds) if you look in the newspaper. In fact, you can look at bond prices every day in the *Wall Street Journal*'s section C. The most complete listing is the *Treasury Bonds, Notes and Bills* table, which shows the previous day's prices for outstanding issues. The two bonds in Table 5.1 are listed as they appear in the *Journal*. CHG denotes the change in the bond's price from the day before. RATE is the fixed interest rate, MATURITY represents the end of its lifespan, and YIELD is its rate of

TABLE 5.1   Bid/Ask Listings as They Appear in the *Wall Street Journal*

Rate	Maturity Mo/Yr	Bid	Asked	Chg	Ask Yld
3⅞	Feb 13	102:02	102:03	3	3.62
5⅜	Feb 31	110:29	110:30	5	4.67

return. We'll discuss these last three terms in the next few chapters. Now that we've got the basics of pricing covered, it's time to discuss accrued interest.

Accrued Interest

When you're buying or selling most types of bonds, *accrued interest* is included in the price. Accrued interest is exactly as it sounds—it's the interest that accumulates (or accrues) each day between payment dates. Accrued interest isn't difficult to calculate. Here's how you do it:

Accrued interest = Annual interest × (number of days ÷ 360)

Since bond interest is paid only twice each year, chances are you won't sell a bond on either of those dates. That's why accrued interest is important. For instance, if you sell a bond one month before the next payment date, you still receive the interest earned for the preceding five months. That's because you're entitled to the sale price *plus* any interest you've earned up to the day before the new owner takes possession of your security. Of course, it cuts both ways—if you are the buyer, you have to pay the purchase price plus five months of accrued interest to the seller. Is that fair? Yes! Because the buyer will receive the full six-month interest payment even though he or she has only owned the bond for one month.

If you're a stock investor, you might be thinking, "Hey, wait a minute! If I sell a stock before its ex-date" (at least two to three weeks before quarterly dividends are paid), "I don't get a partial dividend." That's true, because stocks *trade flat.* In other words, there's no such thing as an accrued dividend. The only time a bond trades flat is when an issuer defaults.

chapter six

MATURITY

The Bare Essentials

- Unlike a stock, a bond has a predetermined lifespan known as its *maturity*.
- Many fixed-income securities never reach maturity due to early redemption features known as *calls* and *puts*.
- Callable bonds may be redeemed by the issuer prior to maturity, while putables provide that option to the bondholder.

Many investors consider bonds to be long-term holdings compared to stocks. Although that might reflect investment behavior, it's an ironic way to represent the inherent nature of each security. After all, bonds have finite lifespans, but equities are perpetual. That's why you could inherit stocks that were purchased 75 years ago, but not bonds.

A bond's predetermined lifespan is commonly known as its *maturity*. Most bond maturities range between 2 and 30 years, although there are some 40-year and even some 100-year bonds outstanding. Securities that mature in less than one year are considered *money market instruments*, 1- to 5-year bonds are *short-term*, 5- to 12-year issues are *intermediate-term*, and bonds maturing in more than 12 years are considered *long-term* (see Figure 6.1).

Bond Maturity

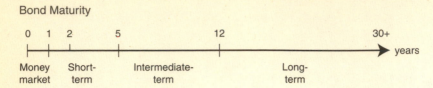

FIGURE 6.1 Bond Maturity Timeline

Large new bond issues usually feature several different maturities. These are known as *serial bonds*. For instance, they could consist of four different maturities, say, 2-, 5-, 10- and 20-year bonds. New issues offered with only one maturity are known as *term bonds*.

Whatever the maturity, a bond's life ends on its *maturity date*, which is when the bond (you guessed it) *matures*. Then the final interest payment and principal are distributed, effectively terminating the obligation of the borrower (issuer) to the lender (investor).

Early Redemption Features

Many fixed-income securities never reach maturity because early redemption features are embedded in their structures. These bonds either contain a *call* or, less commonly, a *put*. Call and put provisions are disclosed in the bond indenture and prospectus (did you read it?) upon issuance and do not change for the life of the security. Since *callable bonds*, or simply *callables*, give issuers more flexibility, their issuance easily outnumbers that of putable securities.

Callables

Callables grant the issuer the right to retire a bond beginning on a specific date. Since this is advantageous for the issuer, but not for the bondholder, it's known as *call risk*. In the same way a mortgage refinancing lowers your borrowing costs, a bond is called when the issuer has an opportunity to refinance its debt at a lower rate. Although this benefits the issuer, investors are not as fortunate because bonds are usually called only after interest rates have fallen. For that reason, after your principal is repaid, you're faced with the less attractive option of reinvestment at a lower rate. That's called *reinvestment risk*. This might not seem like a risk to you since—what's the big deal?—you get your money back. But if you're retired and depend on high interest income, the inability to replace it at a comparable rate is a real matter of concern.

Bondholders are typically given 30 days' notice when a bond is called. (You've got no choice in the matter anyway but, hey, it's the polite thing to do.) Usually an issuer doesn't have the right to call a bond for a certain number of years. For example, if a bond isn't callable for 10 years from its original issue date, then it's said to have 10 years of *call protection* (see Figure 6.2).

Although call characteristics usually vary by bond type, most callable issues retain par calls. That means if the bond is redeemed before maturity, you receive the same amount of principal that would've been paid at maturity. Some bonds with early redemptions feature calls with slight premiums. For instance, you could receive 102 on the call date instead of par ($1,020 instead of $1,000). Some callable issues even have multiple call dates. In that case, investors receive slightly decreasing premiums to par as the bond approaches maturity. In effect, the earlier the bond is subject to redemption, the more an issuer compensates bondholders for the privilege. For example, let's say you bought a 20-year callable bond. Its *call schedule* could read as follows: In 10 years it's callable at 102, in 12 years at 101, and thereafter at par.

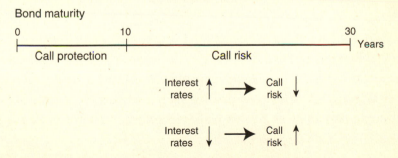

FIGURE 6.2   30-Year Bond with 10 Years of Call Protection

Put Bonds and Sinkers

Putables enable you to get into the driver's seat since you're able to request, or "put," the bonds back to the issuer. It's an effective way to offset re-investment risk because a put bond allows you to redeem the security at par before maturity. In most cases, issuers allow these bonds to be redeemed *only on* specific dates. Not *after*, like callables.

If a put bond is trading below par on its put date, you'll have the opportunity to redeem it at par and reinvest your principal at a higher rate of return. What's the catch? These bonds pay less interest than comparable (nonputable) fixed-income securities. And before you start looking for them, remember that putables are much harder to come by than callables.

An early redemption feature that's also become scarce is the *sinking fund* provision. The issuers of sinking fund bonds, or *sinkers*, have an amount of money designated to redeem a certain number of bonds on a periodic basis before final maturity. Bonds selected for redemption are usually determined by lottery. Consequently, unlike callables, you never know when your bond could be redeemed. Additionally, the redemption price (usually par) might be lower than its secondary market price. A related structure is known as the *pro-rata sinker*, which stipulates an equal percentage of bonds to be redeemed are spread among all investors, instead of by lottery.

Bullet Securities

Bonds devoid of any early redemption features are known as *bullet securities*, commonly referred to as *bullets*—as in straight to one destination: the maturity date. These bonds typically are offered at lower rates (in other words, they're more expensive than comparable callables). But you might be willing to give up higher incremental returns in exchange for call protection through maturity.

chapter seven
COUPON

The Bare Essentials

🍀 A bond's stated annual interest rate is known as its *coupon*.

🍀 Although the coupon represents an *annual* rate, interest is usually paid *semiannually*. Bonds that do not make interest payments are known as *zero coupon bonds*.

🍀 Reinvesting interest payments generates *interest-on-interest*, which illustrates the *power of compounding*.

🍀 The amount that a sum of money in the future is worth today is known as *present value. Future value,* on the other hand, is what your money today would be worth at some point in the future.

Over 20 years ago, investors received *bearer bond certificates* printed with coupons that served as proof of ownership. At each scheduled payment date, an investor would clip a coupon and then mail it to the issuer's trustee in exchange for earned interest. There really is a point to this little snatch of history—today, a bond's stated annual interest rate is known as its *coupon*. However, coupon clipping (as it was then known) ended when distribution of these physical certificates was suspended in 1982. This practice was replaced by electronic *book entry*, which means your record of ownership is only reflected on a bank or brokerage statement. Additionally, interest payments are now distributed directly to bondholders by mail or deposited into investment accounts.

Even if your bond trades at a premium or a discount, the coupon doesn't change. The coupon rate is also known as the *nominal yield*, yet it's rarely referred to that way. To determine the amount of a bond's annual interest, multiply its par value by its coupon.

For example, let's say you consider purchasing a four-year bond with a 5.0 percent coupon offered at 98. Since you're a procrastinator, it takes you two weeks to make up your mind, but by then the price has risen to 102. Without taking out a calculator, what would be the difference between the amount of interest you would've received if you bought the bonds at 98 rather than at 102? Answer: There is no difference. Since the coupon is fixed to the par value of the security, it generates $50 in annual income ($1,000 × 5.0 percent = $50). Although the coupon is an *annual* rate, bond interest is paid *semiannually*. Divide the coupon in half to arrive at the dollar amount you'd receive every six months. As a result, this 5 percent bond that generates $50 annually would pay $25 in interest twice each year (see Figure 7.1).

Semiannual payment dates are dictated by the maturity, *not* the issuance date. For example, if a bond matures on March 26, then you receive interest payments every year on September 26 and March 26.

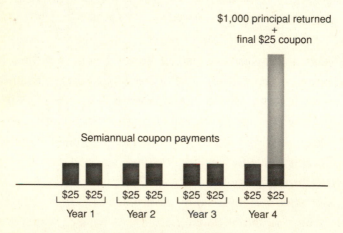

FIGURE 7.1   **Four-year Bond with 5 Percent Coupon**

However, it's not uncommon for a bond to be issued with less than six months remaining to one of these dates. So if this bond was issued on October 10, your *first* interest payment would instead approximate 5½ months of interest. This is known as a *short coupon*.

Zero Coupon Bonds

Although most bonds have coupons, some fixed-income securities don't generate any interest payments. These securities are appropriately called *zero coupon bonds*, or simply *zeros*. Since zeros are still considered debt like their coupon-paying counterparts, investors continue to earn semi-annual interest.

You're probably thinking, "How can you earn interest but not receive an interest payment?" Good question. Instead of receiving a payment every six months, earned interest accrues to the face value of the bond until it matures at $1,000 par value. That's why these securities are also known as *accrual bonds*. Additionally, since zeros don't make coupon payments, they shield investors from reinvestment risk.

Zeros are issued at a deep discount to par because the money you receive at maturity includes the principal *and* the total interest you've earned. For example, although coupon-paying bonds are issued at $1,000, a zero could be issued at, say, $650. Think of it this way—if the bond were instead issued at par, the total amount repaid at maturity would be far greater than par value.

Zero bond interest is characterized as *phantom income*—as in "invisible." Unfortunately, it's not invisible enough—accrued interest from most zero bonds is taxed as if you had actually received it that year. In other words, it's treated as interest income, just like payments from a regular coupon-paying security.

Let's look at an example. Say you're comparing two five-year bonds of equal credit quality that feature the same rate of interest. One is a coupon-paying bond at $1,000 par, and the other is a zero coupon offered

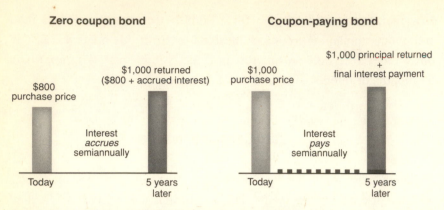

FIGURE 7.2 Zero Coupon Bond versus Coupon-paying Bond

at $800. Given a stable interest rate climate, the regular bond trades near its offering price, generates semiannual interest, and repays face value at maturity. Meanwhile, the zero's semiannual phantom income is reinvested and applied to the principal until it progressively matures at par. Either way, you have a $1,000 principal for each bond at maturity. Different starting point, same ending (see Figure 7.2).

It's important to keep in mind, however, that zero coupon securities only appreciate in a straight line *theoretically*. That is, even if you bought a zero at $800 and you're reporting phantom income each year, adverse market conditions could cause your bond to trade below the purchase price.

Compound and Simple Interest

Did you ever hear about the *power of compounding*? Did you ever wonder what it was? Well, here goes—when you receive interest, you could reinvest it and—are you ready?—start generating interest on your interest. For example, suppose you bought 100 bonds with a 5 percent coupon six months ago and just received the first $2,500 semiannual interest payment. Instead of buying that new bauble you've had your eye on, you reinvest the money at the same rate. By the time the next bond interest payment is received, you'll have also earned some *interest-on-interest:*

$100,000 original investment earning 5% = $5,000 (12 months' interest at 5%)

$2,500 semiannual payment earning 5% = $62.50 (6 months' interest)

Now $62.50 may not seem like much compared to your next $2,500 interest payment, but remember, that's just for starters. If you continue to reinvest interest for 15 years, you'll earn even more interest-on-interest. Figure 7.3 illustrates the rewards of compounding. The more you reinvest, the more your principal grows. The more your principal grows, the more interest you generate. Behold! The power of compounding!

Simple interest, by the way, is just that—simple. You get the interest and then spend it or allocate it elsewhere. Since there's no reinvestment, your principal never changes, and neither does the amount of interest income you receive.

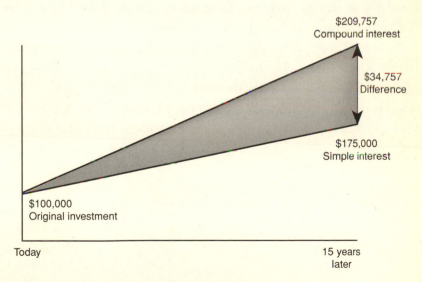

FIGURE 7.3   **Compound versus Simple Interest**

Present and Future Value

You just won the lottery. How much? $25 million dollars! Congratulations! When you bought the ticket you had a choice: take the winnings as a lump sum, or receive it over the next twenty years. You chose the lump sum. So you go down to the lottery office and they take a picture of you and your family holding an oversized $25,000,000 check with your name on it. After the photo op they present you with a normal-sized check for $7.5 million. You say, "Hey! This is nearly $17.5 million short!" "I'm sorry," they reply, "but that's the *present value* of your prize. If you had not chosen a lump sum, you would've received $1.25 million annually for the next twenty years. You see, $25 million represents the *future value* of your winnings."

It might've been a rude surprise, but think of it this way—you still get $7.5 million. Not bad considering you only paid a dollar for that ticket. It also introduces the two elements of an important concept: the *time value of money*. Essentially, the amount that a sum of money in the future is worth today is known as *present value*. *Future value*, on the other hand, is what your money today would be worth at some point in the future. Both present value and future value assume a specified rate of return.

Now let's get back to that prize—why'd you only get $7.5 million? Here's how it works. The lottery officials used an interest rate—in this example 5 percent—and worked backward. Essentially, they took out their financial calculators and figured out what amount of money you'd need today that would produce $25 million in 20 years at a 5 percent

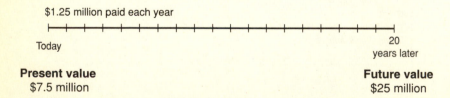

FIGURE 7.4 Present Value and Future Value

compounded rate of interest. They used future value to determine present value (see Figure 7.4).

You could apply this to your own investment goals. For instance, suppose you wanted $50,000 10 years from now and were able to lock in a 5 percent rate of interest. If you had a financial calculator, you could quickly determine that you'd have to invest $30,734 today to reach your goal. But don't worry about doing the calculation—the point of this discussion is to reinforce the importance of compounding (behold!) since reinvested interest is an important theme in fixed-income investing.

chapter eight
YIELD

The Bare Essentials

* Unlike the rigid nature of a bond's coupon, or *nominal yield,* other yields are constantly in flux.
* *Yield-to-maturity* calculates the percentage rate of return assuming interest payments are reinvested at the same coupon rate and the bond is held to maturity. *Yield-to-call* is used for bonds with early redemptions, and *yield-to-worst* is the lower of the two, or the lowest yield you could expect to receive.
* Yield calculations allow us to compare different bonds on a level playing field.

Yield is one of the most commonly used *and* one of the most misunderstood terms in the bond market. So let's get one thing straight—YIELD is not related to STOP signs. But seriously, folks, bond investors commonly get yield all wrong. That's because there are several different kinds of yield that are closely related. Knowing the differences between them will help prevent some costly investment mistakes.

We're going to discuss the four most common types of yield: current yield, yield-to-maturity, yield-to-call, and yield-to-worst. These enable us to fairly compare the value of bonds with different maturities and coupons. In effect, it puts different bonds on the same playing field—

apples-to-apples, if you will. Calculating yields requires a little bit of math because, unlike the rigid nature of a bond's coupon, or *nominal yield*, other yields are constantly in flux.

That said, let's start with *current yield*. Just divide the coupon by par value and then multiply it by the purchase price. For instance, a 7.5 percent bond offered at par would have a current yield of 7.5 percent:

$$\frac{7.5}{100} \times 100 = 7.5\%$$

That one was easy, especially if you noticed that the current yield at par is equal to the coupon rate. It's doubtful, however, that you'll find bonds trading exactly at par. So let's use the same 7.5 percent coupon, but assume the bond is trading at 102. The current yield would be calculated as follows:

$$\frac{7.5}{102} \times 100 = 7.35\%$$

Even though current yield is often quoted, it's not an accurate measure of value since it doesn't incorporate the future stream of interest payments or the difference between the purchase price and redemption value. That's why we use *yield-to-maturity* (YTM). Why did I waste your time with current yield? Because—mark my words—one day someone's going to insist current yield is all you need. You'll know better.

When someone in the bond business mentions "yield," they're most often referring to YTM, which usually accompanies an offering description. Yield-to-maturity is the percentage rate of return assuming a bond is held until maturity and interest payments are reinvested at the same nominal yield. Yield-to-maturity integrates any difference between par value and the actual price you paid. Now that's a mouthful. To calculate it, just insert the appropriate numbers into the following equation:

$$P = \sum_{t=1}^{2n} \frac{C/2}{\left(1 + \dfrac{r}{2}\right)^t} + \frac{R}{\left(1 + \dfrac{r}{2}\right)^{2n}}$$

Just kidding. No one in their right mind would do this longhand any-more—we use financial calculators or plug the numbers into software that's installed on our computers.

Since YTM accounts for the difference between a bond's cost and how much you'll be paid at maturity, some assumptions could be made without doing any math:

- When a bond is trading at par, YTM is equal to its current yield and coupon.

- When a bond is trading at a discount, YTM is greater than the coupon.

- When a bond is trading at a premium, YTM is lower than the coupon.

Let's take an example. If you bought a 10-year bond at par with a 6 percent coupon, you could safely assume that YTM is 6 percent. Now suppose you bought the bond at 97. When your bond is redeemed at par, you'd have to account for a 3-point gain, or $30. As a result, you could assume that YTM would be greater than 6 percent—in fact it's 6.4 percent. Now what if the same bond were purchased at 102? If you assumed that YTM would be lower than the coupon rate, you'd be right—it's 5.7 percent.

But wait! If you bought a callable bond, wouldn't YTM provide you with an incomplete assessment of its potential return? After all, how could you possibly rely on its YTM if it could be redeemed long before the maturity date? For that reason, you should use the bond's *yield-to-call* (YTC). As the name implies, YTC is the same calculation as YTM, except it targets a call date instead of the maturity date. If there's more than one call date, multiple YTC calculations should be made. Yield-to-call incorporates the future stream of reinvested coupon payments, the price paid for the bond, and the price you would receive at each early redemption date.

Yield-to-worst (YTW) is exactly what it sounds like—it's the lowest yield you can receive. No fancy arithmetic here—just pick the lower of a bond's YTM and YTC. This is the most conservative way to view a bond's potential return and should *always* be assessed when purchasing any callable security.

Putting YTM in Perspective

Here's the good news—the power of compounding is alive and well (Behold!). The bad news? In reality, yield calculations just are not reliable indicators of potential total return. For instance, suppose you purchased 100 10-year bonds at 98 with a 6 percent coupon and 6.28 percent YTM. The YTM calculation assumes that you will reinvest every $3,000 semi-annual payment at the same 6 percent coupon rate and compound that interest until maturity. In other words, it assumes you didn't spend any of it. Now be honest—does that sound realistic to you?

You see the problem here? If you don't reinvest every interest payment, your rate of return is going to be lower than the YTM calculation. But let's suppose you decide to be a good camper and reinvest every interest payment along the way. There's still a problem—you can't predict what interest rates will be in the future. You could reinvest at 3 percent, then at 5 percent, and then at 2 percent over the next 10-year span. Who knows? What we *can* predict with certainty is that you won't be able to reinvest each of those 20 payments at the same rate of interest.

This might not seem like a big problem to you because your interest payments don't change. However, since a bond's total return is commonly expressed as YTM, it's important to understand the consequences of these underlying assumptions. And by the way, there is an exception—zero coupon bonds automatically compound interest at the same rate for the life of the security.

So what's the real value of YTM? It allows you to quantify and compare different bonds by putting them on the same playing field. When we discuss transactions in the last section, you'll learn how to calculate *total return*, which accurately measures what you really earned.

Basis Points

Basis points provide us with a way to articulate exact differences in bond yields. That's because each basis point represents 1/100th of a percent

(100 basis points equal 1 percent). Bond analysts regularly express basis points in shorthand, either as *bp* or *bps*.

As we discussed earlier, yield—not price—is the most effective way to put different types of bonds on the same playing field. Consequently, being able to discuss yield differences in basis points allows us to more accurately assess value. For example, what's the difference in yield between a bond trading at 7 percent YTM and a bond trading at 4.5 percent YTM? Well, since 7 percent is equivalent to 700 basis points and 4.5 percent is equivalent to 450 basis points, the yield differential is 250 basis points.

Additionally, a *percentage change* is not the same as a *change in yield*. For example, if a bond was offered at 4 percent a month ago but is now trading at 5 percent, the yield has risen by 100 basis points. However, it has not changed by 1 percent. Huh? That's because the *percentage change* is actually 25 percent. Don't believe me? Just divide 1 by 4. That's why it makes more sense to use basis points.

chapter nine
CREDIT QUALITY

The Bare Essentials

* *Credit rating agencies* provide us with the most effective way to objectively gauge bond issuer risk.

* *Moody's Investors Service* (Moody's), *Standard & Poor's* (S&P), and *Fitch Ratings* (Fitch) are the three leading agencies that evaluate credit quality and then assign ratings to bond issuers.

Suppose you apply for a credit card. The card company submits your application to a credit agency that reviews your past spending habits and the debt you currently owe. Finally, a personal credit score is produced, which essentially ranks your ability to pay back debt. The card company uses the score to determine whether your application should be accepted and, if it is, also uses the ranking to set your credit limit.

Wouldn't it be helpful if we had access to the same type of independent analysis every time we considered extending a loan to a bond issuer? Even though bond issuers are bound to have varying degrees of risk, few of us have the resources, skills, or (more importantly) the desire to thoroughly tear apart a company's balance sheet. What are you supposed to do, get a degree in financial analysis before you buy a bond? A finance degree sure wouldn't hurt. But rest assured, Virginia, there are companies that provide us with this analysis. The views of these *credit rating agencies* are crucial to investors and issuers alike.

The three major rating agencies are *Moody's Investors Service* (Moody's), *Standard & Poor's* (S&P), and *Fitch Ratings* (Fitch). In 1975, each of them was designated a Nationally Recognized Statistical Rating Organization (NRSRO) by the SEC. Champagne and accolades were shared. Truth be told, since the fixed-income market pays closest attention to Moody's and S&P, you'll discover that most bond offerings typically exclude Fitch ratings.

All three NRSROs are independent companies that are paid fees by bond issuers to evaluate their financial profiles. Now that might seem like a classic case of asking the wolf to protect the chicken coop, but it's not. All agencies are closely monitored by the SEC and are expected to produce unbiased research opinions.

Each rating agency has developed a ranking system that allows you to quickly assess an issuer's financial strength. Same as a bank or credit card company would do to you. In fact, it's the most effective way for investors to objectively gauge the risk of a bond issuer. These rankings also provide us with a way to track the ongoing health of a company because rating analysts closely follow them.

Credit ratings are determined by a number of factors, such as total amount of outstanding debt, stability and growth of revenue, and balance sheet flexibility. Most importantly, ratings enable us to quantify default risk by providing a forward-looking analysis of an issuer's ability to make timely interest payments and return principal at maturity.

We'll talk more specifically about what these credit ratings are—and the consequences of changes to an issuer's rankings—when we discuss corporate bonds in Part 4. For now, let's just say that the highest rating awarded by all three agencies is Triple-A.

The rating systems are not fault-proof. In fact, after a spate of corporate defaults took the agencies by surprise in 2001 and 2002, their analysis became even more rigorous. Despite any shortcomings, these ratings have been an invaluable tool for bond investors. And let's face it, outside of hiring your own group of analysts or becoming one yourself, there's no better gauge available.

PART THREE
Simplifying Key Concepts

chapter ten

WHY BAD NEWS IS GOOD NEWS

The Bare Essentials

- *Inflation* occurs when spending has increased relative to supply—think of it as too much money chasing too few goods.

- The most widely watched inflation barometer is the *Consumer Price Index,* or *CPI.*

- Since a bond's coupon rate does not change, inflation erodes the future value of its fixed-income stream.

- Strong economic growth typically generates higher interest rates and depresses bond prices—so what's bad for the economy (slower growth) is usually good for bond investors.

You've all heard about inflation—it's bandied about by television news anchors, featured in newspapers, and occasionally appears on the front cover of business magazines. Inflation even surfaces unknowingly in casual conversation. For instance, did your parents ever complain about the cost of going to the movies today? And then proceed to reminisce that it used to cost 50 cents and candy bars were a nickel? Well, whether you realized it or not, they were commenting on inflation.

When the cost of a product or service rises and its quality remains the same, that's *inflation*. Get it?—prices *inflate*. It usually occurs when spending has increased relative to supply—think of it as too much money chasing too few goods. The opposite of inflation is *deflation*. In a deflationary environment, prices decline over a long period of time. Deflation occurs infrequently in healthy economies since inflation is a natural byproduct of growth. Be careful not to confuse deflation with *disinflation*. That's when progressively lower rates of inflation occur, usually due to an economic slowdown or surge in productivity. In other words, prices continue to rise, but at a slower pace.

The most widely watched inflation barometer is the *Consumer Price Index* (CPI), which is expressed as year-over-year growth, or the percentage change compared to the previous year. Although the U.S. inflation rate has been fairly modest during the last 10 years—ranging between 1 and 4 percent—it rose as high as 14 percent in 1980. Despite economic growth, inflation is harmful to consumers since rising prices cause our *cost of living* to escalate. When the cost of living escalates, our *spending*—or *purchasing*—*power* is diminished.

For example, let's say you loaned a friend $1,000. I know what you're thinking—that better be a *good* friend. Anyway, your friend is going to pay you back in 12 months. Exactly one year later, your friend shows up with $1,000 in small, nonsequential, unmarked bills (she's been watching too many movies). Nevertheless, the full amount is repaid. But if inflation rose by 3 percent in the interim, then that $1,000 loan you provided one year ago is actually worth $970 today.

Of course, when it comes to family and friends, nobody really thinks to compensate for inflation. But when it comes to fixed-income investments, you should. For instance, if a 10-year bond nominally yields 5.5 percent and you subtracted a 3 percent inflation rate, the *real interest rate* would be 2.5 percent. Since 2.5 percent represents the increase in your spending power above and beyond the eroding effects of inflation, it's a more accurate way to portray the bond's rate of return.

Inflation causes interest rates to rise because investors want to be compensated for eroding future returns. If rates were unchanged, inves-

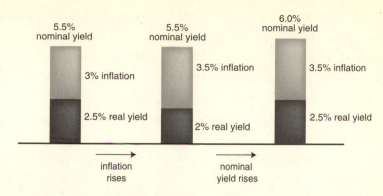

FIGURE 10.1   Inflation and Real Yields

tors would be faced with a lower real rate of interest. Let's go back to the previous example—what would happen if inflation were 3.5 percent instead? That's right—the real yield would drop from 2.5 percent to 2.0 percent (see Figure 10.1). Now let's take it a step further. If rising inflation causes the real rate of return to deteriorate, bond investors naturally demand higher nominal yields to compensate for this loss.

You get the idea. That's why inflation triggers a negative reaction from the bond market—bonds pay a fixed rate of interest, but inflation reduces the future value of their coupons. By extension, the value of the anticipated stream of income payments declines, leaving you with a lower rate of return.

In reality, investors tend to demand higher average real yields when inflation expectations are rising, and accept lower average real yields when inflation expectations are receding. It all works out pretty well as long as the *actual* rate of inflation approximates what's embedded in the nominal rate. That's why the fixed-income market reacts so strongly to a surprisingly high or low CPI that is not a close approximation of what's already been reflected by bond yields. Unfortunately, accurate inflation forecasts are the exception, not the rule. So when the CPI is reported, the bond market jumps. Or breathes a sigh of relief.

The detrimental effect that inflation could inflict on your future purchasing power is especially important to consider if you're saving for your retirement. Although Social Security payments have a built-in cost-of-living adjustment that accounts for inflation each year, you're not afforded the same luxury with fixed coupons.

So why is bad news good news? Well, think of it this way—a slower economy may be bad news for corporate earnings and government coffers, but the resulting drop in overall demand eases inflation pressures. Decreased demand and lower inflation, in turn, translate to higher real rates of return for bondholders. And, as we'll learn in the following section, lower inflation facilitates lower interest rates and lifts bond prices.

chapter eleven
BOND PRICES AND INTEREST RATES

The Bare Essentials

🍀 When interest rates decline, bond prices rise.

🍀 When interest rates rise, bond prices decline.

Peanut butter and jelly. Ham and cheese. Spaghetti and meatballs. Bond prices and interest rates. How could anyone think of one without thinking of the other?

All right, maybe you didn't think of that last one, but you get the point—when you think of bond prices, you should automatically think about interest rates. As we all know, interest rates are constantly in flux, rising and falling due to a variety of economic and market factors. Since bonds are so closely related, when interest rates are volatile, bonds prices are bound to be volatile as well.

To understand the connection between interest rates and bond prices, we need to start with the coupon. Although variables that dictate coupon rates shift in priority, prevailing interest rates are always a major factor. So—all else being equal—when interest rates fall, newly created bonds are issued with lower average coupons than comparable securities that were issued in a higher-rate environment. Consequently, demand for older (outstanding) bonds traded in the secondary market increases since their coupons are likely to be higher, causing prices to appreciate.

However, if interest rates were to rise, newly issued bonds would have more appeal since coupon rates would also rise. Since fixed-income securities issued in the lower-rate environment become less attractive, demand drops, causing outstanding bond prices to decline.

These examples illustrate how bond prices and interest rates are *inversely* correlated. Here's the cardinal law: *When interest rates decline, bond prices rise; when interest rates rise, bond prices decline* (see Figure 11.1).

If you're confused, take comfort—this inverse relationship initially seems counterintuitive to most investors. However, you're going to have great difficulty understanding the basic mechanics of the fixed-income market if you're unable to get a firm grasp on this concept. A couple of examples should provide some clarity. Suppose you bought a 10-year bond two years ago at par with a 5 percent coupon. Today, the same company issues another 10-year bond with identical characteristics. Interest rates, however, have declined, so the new bond is issued with a 4 percent coupon. Who's happier—issuer or investor? The answer might seem obvious, but it's also instructive. Although the issuer lowered its borrowing costs by 1 percent, it's obvious that investors would prefer 5 percent to 4 percent. Since demand for the older bond would rise, it'll trade at a premium—say, at 102.

Now suppose inflation fears accelerated and interest rates rose. The issuer would be compelled to offer new bonds at higher rates, perhaps, 6 percent. Consequently, the appeal of your 5 percent coupon drops along with the bond's principal value. When this occurs, the 5 percent bond

FIGURE 11.1   Bond Prices and Interest Rates

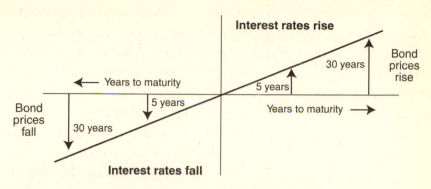

FIGURE 11.2   Impact of Interest Rates on Short and Long Maturities

that was issued at par would be trading at a discount, say, at 98. By the way, discount bond prices are more sensitive when rates rise than premium bonds, which trade above par. That's why premium issues also are known as *cushion bonds*—their higher coupon rates cushion the downward pressure on bond prices.

As a rule of thumb, the longer a bond's maturity, the more its price will change when interest rates fluctuate. Take a look at Figure 11.2. It illustrates the potential price changes of an issuer's 5-year and 30-year bonds as interest rates rise and fall. Now don't let all those lines and arrows intimidate you. It might look complicated, but if you take your time, you will clearly see how the price of a 5-year security is less volatile than its 30-year counterpart.

chapter twelve

MEASURING VOLATILITY

The Bare Essentials

- *Duration* is a measure of the *sensitivity* of a bond's price to interest rate fluctuations.

- Although duration is a complicated concept, the most important part to remember is fairly straightforward—it represents the *percentage change* in a bond's price given a 1 percent rise or fall in interest rates.

There sure have been plenty of ups and downs in the financial markets over the last decade. In fact, there's been as much volatility recently as we've witnessed at any time in modern history. Fortunately, fixed-income investments tend to be less volatile than equities—meaning that price swings, on average, are less dramatic. But just because bonds are less volatile than stocks doesn't preclude the need to understand how volatility affects fixed-income investments.

As we learned in the last chapter, interest rates directly impact bond prices. The effect of fluctuating rates on prices is known as *interest rate risk*. To measure the potential volatility caused by moves in interest rates, bond investors use *duration*. Although it logically might appear that the word "duration" is synonymous with "maturity," it has an entirely different meaning to bond investors: Maturity is a measure of *how long* it will be before the issuer repays the principal; duration, on the other hand, is a measure of *how sensitive* a bond's price is to changes in interest rates.

In short, duration is calculated similarly to yield-to-maturity except that duration also integrates the present value of a bond's future cash flows, weights them according to when they're paid, and then expresses the result in years. It includes the coupon amount, time remaining to call date, and the length of final maturity. Here's the equation so you can calculate it at home:

$$D = \frac{\sum\limits_{t=1}^{m} \dfrac{tC_t}{(1+r)^t}}{\sum\limits_{t=1}^{m} \dfrac{C_t}{(1+r)^t}}$$

If you didn't get that doctorate in mathematics, shame on you. But fear not, even though this is one of the most complex concepts in the bond market, we can skip the detailed mathematical analysis. That's because the most important thing to remember has nothing to do with how duration is calculated. You just need to understand how it's applied: *Duration represents the percentage change in a bond's price given each 1 percent rise or fall in interest rates.*

Duration also assumes that all interest rates—from short-term to long-term—rise or fall by the same amount. This is what's known as a *parallel interest rate shift*. In reality, these parallel shifts do not occur since different maturities are impacted by different factors. Despite the fact that it's an imperfect measure, duration remains the best way to estimate potential bond volatility.

Let's look at an example. If you own a 10-year bond with a 6½-year duration and interest rates fall by 1 percent, the price of your security would rise by approximately 6.5 percent. Conversely, if interest rates were to rise by 1 percent, principal would decline by 6.5 percent. You see the trick here? Look at Figure 12.1 to compare this bond with the volatility of a 30-year bond with a 13-year duration.

Clearly, lower duration produces less price volatility. Let's review one more example just to make sure you've nailed this down. Suppose you expect interest rates to decline in the next 12 months. Which would give

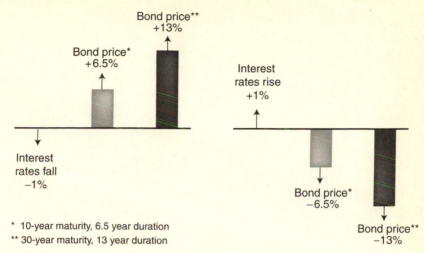

FIGURE 12.1 **Comparing Bond Durations**

you more bang for the buck—a bond with a 2-year duration or an 11-year duration? Good. You chose the longer duration (right?) because each 1 percent downtick in rates would correlate to an 11 percent appreciation in principal. Of course, if you thought interest rates were going to rise, you would buy the bond with the shorter duration to minimize principal depreciation.

The duration of an issue changes over time, especially with callable securities. For instance, suppose 7 years ago you bought a 30-year bond with 10 years of call protection. Its duration was 13 years at the time of issuance. Since then, interest rates have dropped substantially and it's trading at a premium to its par value. That means the bond is now vulnerable to call risk, so duration would be estimated to its call date—with only three years of call protection remaining, it'll have a duration of approximately 1.5 years. On the other hand, if interest rates rose, the bond would trade at a discount and duration would be calculated to maturity.

These are all coupon-paying securities. What about the duration of a zero coupon bond? Let's take say a 15-year zero. Go ahead, do it in your head. Seriously. Give up? 15. Since all future cash flows are received at maturity, the duration of a zero bond is always equal to its maturity—another amazing factoid to feature at your next dinner party.

chapter thirteen
ARMCHAIR ECONOMIST

The Bare Essentials

🍀 There are a handful of economic indicators that are worth watching. Together, they signal important trends that directly impact the bond market.

🍀 Monetary policy wielded by the Federal Reserve (the U.S. central bank) has an enormous impact on the bond market. The federal funds rate is one of the most important tools it uses to influence economic activity.

This is going to be one of the shortest chapters on economics you've ever read. Not because economics is unimportant—it's at the crux of most issues that shape the bond market—but I'd need another 200 pages to do it justice. Perhaps that's a future *Naked Guide.* For now, I've isolated some key topics rather than attempting to cover the entire subject in one chapter.

The state of the economy is important to bond investors because it directly impacts corporate profitability and job creation. By extension, the pace of economic activity affects business and consumer credit demand. Credit demand, in turn, influences the level of interest rates. And as you now know, interest rates affect bond prices.

Economic Indicators

Over 50 economic reports are released each month by government agencies, universities, and consulting firms. But don't worry—most of these are only useful for traders and economists. In fact, following just a handful of reports should quickly allow you to develop a practical understanding of how the economy works and its effect on interest rates.

Among the most important economic indicators are the Consumer Price Index (CPI), which we already discussed; the *Employment Report*, which provides our best insights into the labor market (including the widely reported national unemployment rate); the *Institute of Supply Management* (ISM) *Manufacturing Survey*, a review of activity in over 20 different industries; and the *Retail Sales* report, an important gauge of consumer spending habits. Like all economic indicators, they are each announced on a regular monthly schedule.

For the record—and the inevitable dissenters out there who majored in economics—the four just mentioned, and the ones that follow, were selected on a *subjective* basis. In fact, other than the Employment Report, there's little agreement about which report should take precedence over another. Part of the problem is due to the constantly changing nature of the bond market. For that reason, the relative importance of these releases shifts over time to reflect prevailing economic conditions. But, since the objective of this book is to focus on the bare essentials, I've attempted to isolate the few releases that appear to have the most consistent impact on the bond market.

If you're the type who hungers for even more economic data, knock yourself out—other key monthly releases include *Housing Starts*, *Durable Goods*, *Producer Price Index*, *Industrial Production*, *Consumer Sentiment*, *Trade Balance*, and *Leading Economic Indicators*. The bond market is also sensitive to weekly *Jobless Claims* and the quarterly *Gross Domestic Product* (GDP) report, which provides the broadest measure of recent economic growth (see Table 13.1).

TABLE 13.1 Economic Indicators

U.S. Economic Indicators	Frequency of Release	A Measure of:
Consumer Price Index (CPI)	Monthly	Consumer prices for goods and services (inflation)
Consumer Sentiment	Monthly	Consumer confidence
Durable Goods	Monthly	Manufacturing orders
Employment	Monthly	Trends in the job market and the unemployment rate
Gross Domestic Product (GDP)	Quarterly	Economic output and spending (growth)
Housing Starts	Monthly	Start of construction on single- and multi-family homes
Index of Leading Economic Indicators (LEI)	Monthly	Composite of 10 indicators used to predict economic trends
Industrial Production	Monthly	Output of factories and mining and utility companies
Institute for Supply Management (ISM)	Monthly	Manufacturing activity
Jobless Claims	Weekly	Initial filings for state unemployment insurance
Producer Price Index (PPI)	Monthly	Prices of goods at the business level
Retail Sales	Monthly	Retail and food service consumer spending
Trade Balance	Monthly	Difference between exports and imports

Impact on the Bond Market

The reports just mentioned are responsible for much of the volatility in the bond market. However, it's difficult to know the data that will have the greatest impact ahead of time. Even the most skilled economists can be off the mark. In reality, much of it is about hindsight—the primary market movers are usually the ones that register the biggest surprises. Think about it—how could you know which report is going to be a surprise until after it occurs?

For example, suppose the manufacturing sector is humming along at a moderate pace and the consensus forecasts no change. Then the ISM survey is released and—whoa there!—it reveals that manufacturing activity has suddenly strengthened beyond these expectations. Prospects for a stronger economy follow, which heightens inflation concerns (remember the last chapter?) and causes bond prices to decline. In fact, that's how most economic releases affect the market—bond prices decline when the data is stronger than expected, and rise when it's weaker.

Get it? It's not *whether* manufacturing is weak or strong that causes sudden shifts in the bond market since yields already incorporate consensus expectations. It's the *element of surprise* that's important. This is what causes market volatility, not a number that meets a forecast.

Everyone has an opinion about the economy. Sort of like talking about politics. But try not to get too caught up in all the data—no matter how much you know, forecasting can be more art than science. Nevertheless, tracking the state of the economy does provide important clues about the direction of interest rates. At the very least, you should aspire to be an Armchair Economist (trademark pending). Formal training is not required.

Don't Fight the Fed

No dialogue about the economy would be complete without discussing the Federal Reserve—the central bank of the United States—commonly referred to as *the Fed*. Although every country has its own central bank, the Fed's impact is unparalleled due to the sheer size of the U.S. economy and the vast reach of its capital markets.

The Fed administers monetary policy and has broad regulatory powers over the nation's credit system and money supply. The Federal Reserve actually comprises 12 regional banks (Atlanta, Boston, Chicago, Cleveland, Dallas, Kansas City, Minneapolis, New York, Philadelphia, Richmond, St. Louis, and San Francisco) managed by a board of governors who are appointed by the President for 14-year terms. The President also selects a chairman and vice chairman from among the governors to serve four-year terms (they can be reappointed), although the Senate must confirm them both.

Despite the politics involved in receiving an appointment, Fed governors are autonomous. In fact, even though board members are not appointed for life terms, their independence is akin to members of the U.S. Supreme Court.

When the Fed chairman speaks, the market (and the press) hangs on every word. Market prognosticators usually spend the next couple days analyzing the speech for subtle messages that might provide clues to future Fed action. There simply is no financial figure in the world who receives more attention—you may want to start paying attention, too.

The *federal funds rate*, or simply the *fed funds rate*, is the target interest rate that banks charge each other for overnight loans. It's determined eight times a year by the Federal Open Market Committee (FOMC) in January, March, May, June, August, September, November, and December. The FOMC report is the most widely followed announcement in the bond market. The statement is released at 2:15 P.M. after one or two days of eating jelly doughnuts and discussing the current state of the economy. The FOMC commentary is fairly brief—usually only a few paragraphs—and declares whether the committee is biased towards weakness or strength or feels just about right. Like porridge for the Three Bears.

If the FOMC concludes that the economy could use another shot in the arm, the funds rate is lowered (or *eased*)—this is known as accommodative monetary policy. If inflation fears are percolating, the funds rate is lifted (or *tightened*). And if risks to the economy are considered balanced, the rate remains unchanged. When the funds rate is modified, the Fed usually announces a similar change to the slightly higher *discount rate*. This is the rate a member bank would pay to borrow directly from the Federal Reserve. It is largely symbolic, though, since this credit line would only be tapped as a last resort.

If the funds rate is altered, it's rarely modified by more than 25 to 50 basis points. Now one-fourth to one-half of 1 percent might seem inconsequential to you but, since banks must comply with the target rate, Fed action directly impacts the ebb and flow of credit in the U.S. economy. In other words, when the funds rate is eased, the cost of capital decreases. That gives companies and consumers the incentive to spend more, which sparks economic activity and fosters inflation. When the funds rate is tightened, the higher cost of capital causes a pullback in spending and is disinflationary.

Most economists concede that it requires 9 to 12 months for a Fed rate action to materially affect economic activity. That's why bond investors sometimes underestimate its impact. However, history has repeatedly taught us that accommodative monetary policy inevitably leads to stronger growth, while tighter policy ultimately leads to contraction. For that reason, one of the oldest axioms in the market is *don't fight the Fed.*

chapter fourteen
EVALUATING LIQUIDITY

The Bare Essentials

- *Liquidity* refers to the market's demand for (and supply of) a particular security.
- When a bond is said to have good liquidity, it can be readily converted into cash near the price at which it was last bought or sold. *Illiquid* securities offer higher yields but are not appropriate for investors who plan to sell their holdings prior to maturity.

Liquidity is frequently underestimated or even outright ignored. Yet it significantly impacts both a bond's price and its level of volatility. In fact, poor liquidity is often at the heart of many unpleasant investment surprises.

Liquidity refers to the market's demand for (and supply of) a particular security. When a bond is said to have good liquidity, it can be readily converted into cash near the price at which it was last bought or sold. Federal government bonds and other widely traded issues typically provide investors with the best liquidity. Conversely, small bond issues, debt distributed by infrequent borrowers and older securities typically have poor liquidity.

Sure, we're all buy-and-hold investors in spirit, but what if you wanted to sell your holdings prior to maturity? Remember, unlike the stock market, you've got to locate a bidder before a bond can be sold. That might be difficult for stock investors to comprehend—not because it's complicated, but because it's fundamentally different from equity investing. After all, most stocks can be bought or sold at any time for the latest price quoted on the exchange. However, in the over-the-counter market where most bonds trade, no specialist exists to purchase your security as soon as you've decided to sell it.

Understanding the differences between round lots in the stock market versus the bond market should help clarify why liquidity is important. A *round lot* in the stock market is 100 shares. In the bond market it's not less than *$1 million* in par value—anything less is considered an *odd lot* trade. Need further evidence that institutional investors dominate the bond market? This essentially fosters a bifurcated market with two different price levels. That's why it's imperative individual investors carefully evaluate liquidity—virtually every bond you purchase will be an odd lot order.

Of course, there's nothing you can do about the size of a round lot. But there are ways to position for better liquidity. For example, say you were considering two new par bonds issued by different companies that are both rated Single-A. One is an $800 million issue with a 6 percent coupon from a large industrial company; the other is a $200 million deal with a 6.4 percent coupon offered by an infrequent issuer. Which would you purchase? The 6.4 percent bond certainly looks more attractive, but if you had to liquidate your investment prior to maturity, which one do you think would be *better bid*?

If you needed to sell an *illiquid* security before maturity, it's possible you could offer it to every broker-dealer on Wall Street and hear the same dreaded refrain: *no bid*. As they say in the business, that bond "trades by appointment only." If you're lucky, you might receive a below-market bid—traders call this a *throwaway bid*. That means the trader doesn't have much confidence in the resale value of your security, but is willing to provide minimal liquidity. Desperate investors who absolutely need the cash often take whatever they can get, even if it's far below what they consider to be fair value.

Evaluating liquidity is particularly important when participating in *retail* offerings. Since these types of new issues are directed only at individual investors, they tend to have poor liquidity compared to larger offerings that include institutional participants. Like driving a new car off the dealer's lot for the first time, a retail bond typically drops in value soon after it's issued. Although these bonds usually provide extra yield, be wary unless you're a buy-and-hold investor and understand how infrequently they trade in the secondary market.

Pretty harsh, right? Sure it is, but that's the reality of the bond market. Many bond investors find themselves in this position because they were attracted to the higher yields that usually accompany illiquid securities. That's the silver lining—for the buyer, of course—since poor liquidity often translates into above-average yields. It's a fine trade-off as long as you do it with your eyes wide open and are relatively certain you'll be able to hold onto that bond until maturity. If there's any possibility you'd need that principal prior to its maturity date, resist the temptation to reach for a higher yield and just purchase a shorter-maturity bond that more closely matches your potential needs.

PART FOUR
Mainstays of the Market

chapter fifteen
TREASURY SECURITIES

The Bare Essentials

❧ U.S. Treasury securities (*Treasuries*) are auctioned by the federal government and are widely considered the safest investments in the world.

❧ The three most common types of Treasury securities are *bills* (under 1 year to maturity), *notes* (2 to 10 years), and *bonds* (over 10 years to 30 years).

❧ Treasury yields represent the benchmarks to which all other bonds are compared. The 10-year note is the market's bellwether.

❧ The current yields of the most recently auctioned securities are depicted by the *Treasury yield curve*. These include the 3- and 6-month bills, the 2-, 3-, 5-, and 10-year notes, and the recently suspended 30-year bond.

When you think about Treasury securities, think about Washington D.C. Grand marble monuments, stately office buildings, and money. Boatloads of money. After all, as everyone knows, money doesn't only drive Wall Street.

To feed our Federal trough, the U.S. Department of the Treasury (Treasury Department) issues more bonds than any other government issuer in the United States. In fact, nearly $3.5 *trillion* of Treasury securities are outstanding in 2003. Proceeds from bond sales pay for a variety of expenses, such as military equipment and the salaries of elected officials. If you're a U.S. resident, any interest generated by these bonds is exempt from state and local taxes—though you'll still have to pay federal income taxes.

All Treasury securities are guaranteed by the "full faith and credit" of the U.S. government. In other words, the federal government backs these bonds with all its might—that includes tax receipts and myriad other sources of revenue. Since the United States is by far the largest and most prosperous economy, it's needless to entertain a discussion about the possibility of default. Let's put it this way—U.S. Treasuries represent the safest investments in the world. And that's not patriotism, it's fact—last I checked, non-U.S. residents owned more than of 30 percent of outstanding Treasury issues. That's also why Treasuries are considered to be the capital market's *safe haven*. In fact, investors from around the world significantly increase their Treasury investments when political, economic, or market risk heightens. This trend, which causes yields to become artificially low, is known as the *flight to quality*.

Treasury Auctions

Treasuries are issued at regularly scheduled *auctions* throughout the year. An auction is a virtual event, which means there's no one standing at the front of the room with a gavel. The size and frequency of Treasury auctions vary depending on market demand and the shifting financing needs of the federal government.

A select group of investment firms and banks are key participants in the auction process. These 22 *primary dealers* are required to purchase Treasuries at every auction and provide continuous bids and offers in the secondary market.

To their credit, the Treasury Department and the Federal Reserve have made it easy for individuals to participate directly in auctions. All you have to do is submit a *noncompetitive bid*, which merely specifies how many bonds you want to purchase. In addition to noncompetitive bids, *competitive bids* are also submitted. These bids, mostly from institutional investors, indicate the amount of bonds the buyer is willing to purchase at a specific yield. Unless you are an expert trader, though, it does not make sense to submit a competitive bid. Whatever your bid, the minimum purchase is $1,000.

Not all competitive bids are accepted, but every noncompetitive request is filled. The yields of bonds awarded to noncompetitive bidders are an average of all competitive bids that were accepted. However, when there's a Dutch (or single-price) auction, all investors receive the same yield.

The most convenient way to enter a bid is through *Treasury Direct* (www.treasurydirect.com). There's no charge, but first you'll have to open up an account through the Bureau of Public Debt (800-722-2678) or directly with the Federal Reserve (ask your bank for the phone number of the nearest one). Then you can submit bids online, via mail, or through *Buy Direct* over the phone. Should you decide to redeem Treasuries prior to maturity, the Federal Reserve Bank of Chicago will do it for you on *Sell Direct* (it's all part of the same online system). Of course, you could just ignore all of the above and ask a financial advisor to do it for you.

Refunding announcements provide investors with details about the amount of Treasury supply to expect in the upcoming quarter. A press conference usually occurs on the first Wednesday of February, May, August, and November to announce the schedule. The information is posted on Treasury Direct shortly thereafter, or you could call the toll-free number listed above to hear it over the phone.

Although callable securities are no longer auctioned, some Treasuries with call features still trade in the secondary market. Sometimes, the Treasury Department issues new debt by adding to older issues instead of holding an auction—that's called a *reopening*. When a reopening occurs, new securities retain the same coupon and maturity date as the outstanding issue. This allows the Treasury Department to avoid shortages that would likely accompany smaller auctions while simultaneously improving the liquidity of outstanding issues.

By the way, even though the Treasury Department issues U.S. Savings Bonds, we're not going to feature them in this chapter since they're not actively traded or marketable securities. No, I don't intend to skip them. How could I? U.S. Savings Bonds are widely bought by individual investors. They've got their own chapter later in this book.

Treasury Bills, Notes, and Bonds

The three most common types of Treasury securities are *bills, notes,* and *bonds.* All are sold at $1,000 face value, but each retains a distinct maturity range. Bills are issued for up to 1 year and notes are issued for between 2 and 10 years. (For those of you who pay too much attention to detail, no securities are issued between one and two years.) Bonds range from 10+ years through 30 years. Their original monikers never change—for example, even if a five-year note has nine months left to maturity, it's still called a note. The most recently auctioned Treasuries are considered *on-the-run*, while older issues are considered *off-the-run*.

Treasury bills, colloquially known as *T-bills*, or *bills*, are zero coupon securities sold at a discount to face value. Bills mature in one year or less and are auctioned every week throughout the year. Although one-year bill auctions were suspended in 2001, three other maturities are still issued: 4 weeks, 3 months (13 weeks), and 6 months (26 weeks). The 3-month T-bill yield is commonly used by investment professionals to represent the *risk-free rate of return*.

Unlike other Treasuries, T-bills are always quoted by yield, not price. Since bills pay interest only at maturity, their simple yield (or *discount rate*) represents the difference between the purchase price and final redemption value. Simple yield, however, reflects less than one year of total return. As a result, T-bills should be evaluated by their *bond equiv-*

alent yield (BEY) in order to be accurately compared to the annualized compounded yield of a coupon-bearing security. Bond equivalent yield typically is quoted with the discount rate but, for those of you who like to struggle through a good math equation, here goes:

$$BEY = \frac{365 \times \text{discount rate}}{360 - (\text{days to maturity} \times \text{discount rate})}$$

By the way, the Treasury Department also auctions *cash management bills* in order to supplement the short-term financing provided by T-bills. These are structured similarly to T-bills, but auctions are not regularly scheduled and are held less frequently.

Treasury notes produce semiannual interest and are auctioned in 2-year, 3-year, 5-year and 10-year maturities. Two-year notes are auctioned monthly and three-year notes are sold quarterly. The five-year note is auctioned eight times each year, although four of those auctions are scheduled reopenings. The 10-year note, which is auctioned quarterly, recently became the most widely followed—or *benchmark*—issue in the bond market.

Treasury bonds have maturities beyond 10 years and pay semiannual interest. In a fit of euphoria caused by a temporary federal budget surplus, Treasury bond auctions were suspended in 2001. Actually, only the 30-year maturity was being auctioned at the time. Though no further bond issuance is currently planned, previously auctioned securities continue to actively trade in the secondary market.

Treasury Inflation Protected Securities

Until recently, investors would have been hard-pressed to offset the damaging effects that rising inflation inflicted on their bond portfolios. But you know what they say, "If you can't beat 'em, join 'em." That's exactly what the federal government did—it embraced the enemy and began auctioning *Treasury Inflation Protected Securities*, or *TIPS*, in 1997. These securities are auctioned at $1,000 par value, provide semiannual interest payments, and are issued with a 10-year maturity (the 5-year and 30-year TIPS auctions were suspended). TIPS are also subject to reopenings like other Treasury securities.

TIPS are inflation-indexed bonds designed to *benefit* when inflation rises. Of course, *this is contrary to the way inflation affects other bonds.* Typically, when accelerating inflation causes interest rates to back up, prices of traditional bonds decline. The principal value of TIPS, however, is adjusted daily by a factor tied to the performance of the Consumer Price Index-Urban Consumers (CPI-U), the most comprehensive measure of inflation and usually what you see reported in the media (see Figure 15.1).

There's another twist—even though its coupon is fixed, a TIPS semiannual interest payment will vary depending on its principal value. I know that might sound odd, given that semiannual coupon payments on other bonds never change. The reason is simple: Interest payments on traditional bonds are determined by multiplying the coupon rate by its $1,000 principal value at maturity. However, the interest payment on TIPS is determined by multiplying its fixed coupon by its *daily adjusted principal*. In other words, when a TIPS principal rises due to higher inflation, its interest payments rise as well. For example, let's say you purchase two bonds at $1,000 par value. One is a TIPS with a 4 percent coupon, and the other is a Treasury bond with a 6 percent coupon. Inflation rose in the following months, causing the principal of your TIPS security to appreciate to $1,010 and the principal of your Treasury bond to depreciate to $990. Semiannual interest payments are due. How much interest should you expect to receive from each security?

$$\text{TIPS: } \$1,010 \times 4\% = \$40.40; \ \$40.40 \div 2 = \$20.20$$
$$\text{Treasury bond: } \$1,000 \times 6\% = \$60.00; \ \$60.00 \div 2 = \$30.00$$

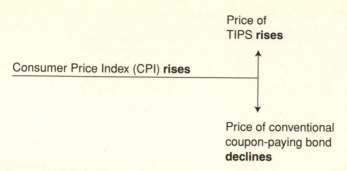

FIGURE 15.1   Impact of CPI on TIPS and Conventional Bonds

Now let's say inflation has receded and the TIPS principal drops to $980 while your Treasury bond rallies to $1,020. Now how much would you expect to receive?

$$\text{TIPS:} \quad \$980 \times 4\% = \$39.20; \quad \$39.20 \div 2 = \$19.60$$

$$\text{Treasury bond:} \quad \$1,000 \times 6\% = \$60.00; \quad \$60.00 \div 2 = \$30.00$$

On the surface, TIPS should yield less than comparable Treasuries as long as there's inflation. You could use simple arithmetic to quickly assess relative value—just subtract the TIPS yield-to-maturity from that of its conventional Treasury counterpart. For example, if a 10-year note yields 5 percent, and a 10-year TIPS yields 3 percent, merely subtract 3 from 5. That means if you think inflation is likely to rise above a 2 percent annual rate during the 10 years that you own the bond, TIPS are likely to outperform the conventional Treasuries.

This straightforward equation is actually one of the most effective ways to gauge the market's current inflation expectations. Think about it—while CPI measures *actual* inflation, an actively traded inflation-indexed bond reflects the *market's inflation expectations*. For bond investors, the latter is as important as the former.

When TIPS mature, their adjusted principal is likely to be higher than par. In fact, unlike other types of fixed-income structures, you could

TABLE 15.1   U.S. Treasury Auction Schedule

U.S. Treasury Security	Auction Schedule
4-week bill	Weekly (usually Tuesday)
3-month (13-week) bill	Weekly (usually Monday)
6-month (26-week) bill	Weekly (usually Monday)
2-year note	Monthly (last Wednesday)
3-year note	Feb, May, Aug, Nov (first Tuesday)
5-year note	Feb, May, Aug, Nov (first Wednesday) *[Reopenings: Mar, Jun, Sep, Dec]*
10-year note	Feb, May, Aug, Nov (first Thursday)
10-year TIPS	Jul (first Wednesday) *[Reopenings: Jan, Oct]*

collect *more* than the $1,000 par value at maturity. On the outside chance deflation occurs, the principal would be adjusted downward. But even if it is adjusted below par at maturity, the Treasury Department promises to pay $1,000 for each bond; heck of a group, those Treasury folk.

Separate Trading of Registered Interest and Principal of Securities

Treasury bills are not the only zero coupon Treasuries available. You could also purchase *Separate Trading of Registered Interest and Principal of Securities*, or STRIPS. They're Treasury securities without coupons—think of them as long-maturity bills. STRIPS, however, are not auctioned.

STRIPS are created by broker-dealers who merely strip (clever, eh?) the coupon from the coupon-paying bond and—voila!—the remaining portion becomes a zero coupon security. Since the underlying issue is still a Treasury, the safety of STRIPS is equivalent to regularly auctioned securities.

The Yield Curve

The Treasury yield curve provides investors with a snapshot of the bond market—you'll spot it in newspapers, in business periodicals, and even on the news. That's because it plots the yield-to-maturity of all on-the-run Treasury securities—from 3- and 6-month bills to 2-, 3-, 5-, and 10-year notes, plus the 30-year bond. Essentially, it's a visual summary of current yields across the entire maturity spectrum.

Normally, the curve has a *positive slope* (Figure 15.2), which shows yields increasing as maturities lengthen. A positive slope is considered normal because uncertainty naturally accelerates as you invest money for longer periods of time. (Think of it this way—it's easier to predict what may happen a few months from now than what may happen in 30 years.) Therefore, investors should be rewarded with progressively higher yields to compensate for bearing more risk.

The positive slope also illustrates that the Federal Reserve is expected to maintain an accommodative stance and investor expectations are sanguine. Life is good.

The yield curve, however, can be turned on its head. This usually occurs when the Federal Reserve tightens monetary policy to put the brakes on a fast-growing economy and creeping inflation pressures. To

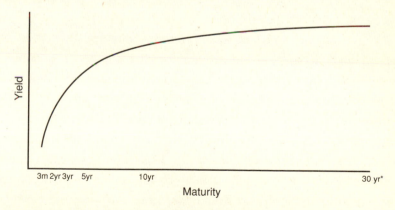

* The last auction of the 30-year Treasury bond was on February 15, 2001.

FIGURE 15.2   Yield Curve with Positive Slope

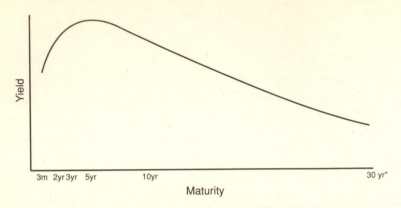

* The last auction of the 30-year Treasury bond was on February 15, 2001.

FIGURE 15.3   Yield Curve with Negative (inverted) Slope

accomplish this, the Fed aggressively raises its short-term funds rate. This produces a *negative slope*, usually called an *inverted yield curve* (see Figure 15.3).

Notice how short maturities are higher than long maturities. As we learned earlier, that's because the Fed can only strong-arm the front end of the curve. Long maturities are impacted by other factors, particularly inflation. Additionally, since an economic slowdown inevitably produces lower interest rates across the curve, long-term investors seek to lock in yields before they decline.

An inverted curve—which is less common and usually short-lived—portends an economic slowdown. You don't have to be an economist to figure that out since, after all, the Fed's intent is to slow economic activity by restraining money supply and dampening credit demand (remember, *don't fight the Fed*). Although Federal Reserve economists do their best not to *overshoot*—or raise the bar too high—these efforts often lead the economy into recession. But hey, at least inflation's under control.

This is why many investors commonly look at the shape of the yield curve for clues to the market's direction. In fact, it's proven to be more reliable than many economic indicators. An inverted curve indicates slower growth, which is typically followed by a bull market for bonds as

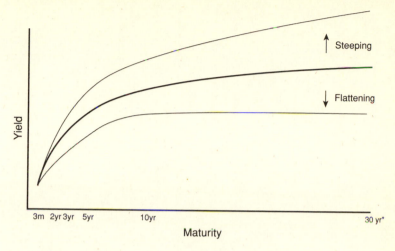

* The last auction of the 30-year Treasury bond was on February 15, 2001.

FIGURE 15.4   Flattening and Steepening Yield Curves

yields decline. On the other hand, a *steep* positive-sloped curve typically occurs after a severe economic slowdown and foreshadows accelerating growth accompanied by higher interest rates. The curve is considered steep when the difference between short- and long-term rates exceeds the historical average. For instance, during the first half of 2003, the spread between the 2-year and the 30-year Treasuries averaged 320 bp. Now that's a steep curve—it's nearly three times its 20-year historical average. By the way, when there's little difference between yields on the curve, it's said to be *flat*. If the spread between long- and short-term yields is shrinking, the curve is said to be *flattening*. Conversely, when the spread starts to widen, the curve is said to be *steepening* (see Figure 15.4).

Although the yield curve is typically associated with U.S. Treasury securities, it's commonly used by financial analysts to depict yields of different maturities in other market sectors. After all, a yield curve is merely a chart of similar bonds of equal quality, from the shortest to the longest maturities. That said, unless otherwise stipulated, it's safe to assume that when the yield curve is mentioned, it's *the* yield curve of U.S. Treasury securities.

chapter sixteen
AGENCY SECURITIES

The Bare Essentials

* Agency securities are issued by federal agencies and privately run corporations known as *government-sponsored enterprises* (*GSE*s) to provide funding for a specific public purpose.

* Agencies are Triple-A rated because they're either explicitly or implicitly guaranteed by the U.S. government.

* *Fannie Mae* and *Freddie Mac* dominate agency issuance. Both are GSEs that facilitate home ownership in the United States.

Pop quiz—what do student loans, farming, and residential housing have in common? Give up? They're all supported by government agencies. Some of these agencies are actually part of the federal branch, while others are government-sponsored corporations that were chartered by Congress to provide funding for a public purpose. Both the federally issued and the government-sponsored types tend to have lengthy formal names, so acronyms and nicknames are commonly used. Bonds issued by these agencies are appropriately called *agency securities*, or simply *agencies*.

Federally issued agencies constitute a negligible amount of outstanding bonds partly because these agencies are able to borrow from the government-owned Federal Financing Bank. You might be familiar with the Government National Mortgage Association, known as *Ginnie Mae* to her friends, which is part of the Department of Housing and Urban Development. This agency purchases mortgage loans and repackages them as mortgage-backed securities. We'll discuss mortgage bonds in the next chapter, so put Ginnie Mae in your back pocket for now.

Federally designated *government-sponsored enterprises* (GSEs) are private sector companies affiliated with, but separate from, the U.S. government. Although there are six active GSE issuers (*Sallie Mae*, however relinquishes its status in 2008), just two—the Federal National Mortgage Association (FNMA, or *Fannie Mae*) and the Federal Home Loan Mortgage Corporation (FHLMC, or *Freddie Mac*)—dominate the agency market. Both of these issuers support the housing market by purchasing mortgage loans from banks and other lenders.

What's that got to do with a public purpose? It's meant to facilitate the "American dream" of owning your own home. By purchasing these loans, Fannie Mae and Freddie Mac free lenders to extend more capital to other borrowers. Subsequently, these housing agencies either earn interest from the loans or repackage them into mortgage securities (that's right, just like Ginnie Mae). The Federal Home Loan Bank—another housing agency—is also a large issuer of agency debt (see Table 16.1).

GSEs are not accorded the same "full faith and credit guarantee" as U.S. Treasuries since they're not part of the federal government, but GSEs are considered implicitly guaranteed because they retain direct credit lines with the U.S. Treasury. As a result, it's unlikely they'd ever be allowed to default. No other bonds—except for Treasuries and securities issued by Federal entities, such as Ginnie Mae—are considered to be of higher quality.

There's been plenty of grumbling recently about the risks posed by the significant amount of debt carried by these corporations. Although the GSEs are certain to face more regulatory scrutiny, it's unlikely that the U.S. government would sever its ties to these companies. After all, can you imagine any politician wanting to lay claim for denying voters access to the American dream?

TABLE 16.1   Most Active Agency Issuers

Government-Sponsored Enterprise (GSE)	Established	Public Purpose	Tax Status
Federal Farm Credit Bank (FFCB) www.farmcredit-ffcb.com	1916	Provides mortgage loans, credit, and services to farmers, rural homeowners, and agricultural cooperatives.	State and local exempt
Federal Home Loan Bank System (FHLB) www.fhlb-of.com	1932	Twelve regional banks regulated by the Federal Housing Finance Board. Facilitates extension of credit to provide access to housing and improve quality of communities.	State and local exempt
Freddie Mac Federal Home Loan Mortgage Corporation (FHLMC) www.freddiemac.com	1970	NYSE-listed corporations that provide a continuous flow of funds to mortgage lenders by purchasing mortgage loans and using them to collateralize mortgage-backed securities. Mandated to promote secondary market for conventional residential mortgages.	Fully taxable
Fannie Mae Federal National Mortgage Association (FNMA) www.fanniemae.com	1938		Fully taxable
Sallie Mae Student Loan Marketing Association (SLMA) www.salliemae.com	1965	NYSE-listed corporation that purchases student loans for private lenders participating in federal student loan programs. Scheduled to relinquish GSE status by 2008.	State and local exempt, except MA, MI, PA, TN
Tennessee Valley Authority (TVA) www.tva.com	1933	Wholly owned corporation of the U.S. government established to develop the Tennessee Valley region.	State and local exempt

Types of Agency Securities

Although agency issuers do not hold auctions, both Freddie Mac and Fannie Mae have regularly scheduled issuance programs that attempt to mirror Treasury benchmark maturities. Additionally, these programs are no longer limited to U.S. dollar issuance—Freddie Mac and Fannie Mae recently began issuing bonds denominated in euros.

Because of the frequency of issuance, low risk of default, and excellent liquidity, bond investors often use agencies as substitutes for Treasuries. However, be aware that—unlike Treasuries—interest generated by some of the most frequent agency issuers is subject to state and local taxes.

The bulk of the agency market comprises coupon-paying securities that pay semiannual fixed rates of interest. These bonds are issued in bullet and callable structures. They're typically sold in minimum increments of $10,000, and in $5,000 multiples thereafter. There are some exceptions—Fannie Mae and Freddie Mac occasionally issue bonds in $1,000 multiples as part of their note programs. And the Federal Home Loan Bank sometimes issues bonds that require a minimum investment of $100,000.

Discount notes, or *discos*, also are issued. They're popular with investors seeking high-quality, short-term alternatives to Treasury bills. That's because they're just like T-bills—they're zero coupon securities issued at a discount to par with up to one year of maturity. Much like STRIPS, longer-term agency zeros are also available.

Another type of agency security is the *step-up note*, or simply *step-up*. Fannie Mae and Freddie Mac issue these securities with maturities that typically do not exceed 15 years. Step-up notes are callable bonds with a unique twist—their coupon rate "steps up" according to a preset schedule over time. This structure provides an effective way to offset interest rate risk since semiannual interest payments continue to rise as long as the security is not called. Be aware, however, that step-ups typically offer only 3 months to 5 years of call protection.

chapter seventeen

MORTGAGE-BACKED SECURITIES

The Bare Essentials

* *Mortgage-backed securities* (MBSs) are bonds secured by real estate. For our purposes, mortgage bonds are backed by residential mortgages.

* The MBS market is comprised of *pass-throughs* and *collateralized mortgage obligations* (CMOs).

* Mortgage bond payments are received monthly and comprise interest and principal.

* Mortgage investors are vulnerable to both *prepayment risk,* which repays principal quicker than expected, and *extension risk,* which returns it slower.

* Since mortgage securities are more complex than any other bond type, it's critically important to fully understand the implications of these investments *before* you invest.

Mortgage-backed securities (MBSs), commonly known as *mortgages,* are bonds secured by real estate. Although the MBS market is less than three decades old, it recently surpassed Treasuries to become the largest sector of the bond market. This is largely due to explosive growth in the housing market and shrinking Treasury supply, although these trends now appear ready to reverse.

Since mortgage bonds are backed by real estate, bondholders have legal claim to the underlying properties pledged as collateral in the event of default. Fortunately, chances of this happening to MBS investors are slim since the bulk of mortgage bonds are issued by housing agencies that retain either a direct or implicit tie to the U.S. government.

The structure of a mortgage bond is much more complex than agency securities, or most other fixed-income securities for that matter. As a result, these bonds carry risks that are unique to the sector and offer higher yields compared to Treasuries. However, since mortgages are fully taxable, some of that yield advantage diminishes. Before we get ahead of ourselves, though, let's discuss how these bonds are created.

Origination

When you take out a mortgage loan to purchase a home, the bank just sits back and collects the interest and principal, right? Well, not really, because the bank has a more productive idea. It takes your loan, packages it together with similar mortgages, and then either sells the collective debt to government housing agencies or broker-dealers. That way, rather than tying up their limited capital, mortgage lenders can use the immediate proceeds to extend credit to other borrowers.

In addition to issuing the majority of agency securities, Fannie Mae and Freddie Mac issue most mortgage-backed bonds. That's because together they own or guarantee over one-third of all U.S. residential mortgages. Ginnie Mae is also a major issuer but, since it provides the additional benefit of a U.S. government guarantee, its bonds yield slightly less than those of both Fannie Mae and Freddie Mac.

Although this sector also comprises commercial mortgage-backed securities, they're typically not offered to individual investors. So we're just going to stick to residential mortgage securities, which include bonds backed by single- and multifamily loans (from one to four families) for houses and apartment dwellings.

But let's back up for a second and return to the point where the lender sells the mortgage loan. When a bunch of mortgages are packaged together, a *pool* is created. Pools typically range from $25 million to $50 million and consist of mortgage loans with similar interest rate and maturity characteristics. For example, a pool could comprise single-family 30-year conventional mortgages paying 6 percent interest.

After an agency or bond dealer purchases a pool, it's split up into smaller pieces that resemble the $1,000 par value familiar to bond investors. Due to an originator's fee, the fixed coupon rate is usually about 50 basis points lower than the underlying mortgage loan in the pool. The new security then serves as a conduit for payments on the collateral (see Figure 17.1).

The stated par value of a mortgage security is pretty much where the similarity to other fixed-income securities begins and ends. Unlike the semiannual interest paid by most other types of bonds, mortgages pay monthly. Why monthly rather than semiannual payments? You could answer that by thinking about your own mortgage. Give up? Mortgage payments are due every month, right? It's those payments that are passed on to bondholders, who receive a pro rata share of the total monthly payments from the pool. Due to this monthly cycle, mortgage bond yields are actually converted to semiannual (bond equivalent) yields to allow for an apples-to-apples comparison with other fixed-income securities.

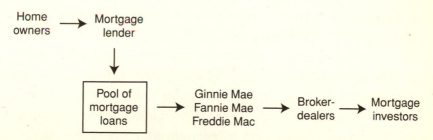

FIGURE 17.1 **Mortgage Bond Origination**

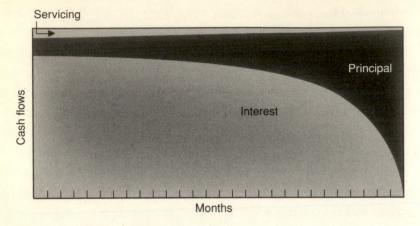

FIGURE 17.2 Mortgage Bond Cash Flow

The composition of those monthly proceeds is also unique. Mortgage securities pay investors both interest *and* principal along the way. (After all, your mortgage payments consist of both interest and principal. Otherwise, you'd never pay off the loan.) So, just like your home loan, mortgage bond payments comprise mostly interest at the beginning, and gradually pay more principal as the security becomes *seasoned.* This is one of the most important differences between mortgage bonds and other types of fixed-income securities—a lump sum of principal is not repaid on a defined maturity date (see Figure 17.2).

Prepayments

The fun doesn't end there, because mortgage bond payments are not fixed. Now why would they go and do that? Once more, it's a function of the underlying collateral. The principal and interest components of mortgage loans are paid according to a specific schedule. In reality, though, most homeowners don't behave that way, so monthly cash flow generated by these bonds varies over time. This is largely due to unscheduled principal payments, also known as *prepayments,* or simply *prepays.*

There are four reasons that prepayments occur. First, when home-owners pay more than the monthly amount that's due, it's applied directly to principal. That's known as a *curtailment*. Second, the mortgage loan could be refinanced. *Refinancing* generally occurs when long-term interest rates begin to decline meaningfully, tempting homeowners to lower borrowing costs by securing lower mortgage rates. When rates drop dramatically in a short period of time, many homeowners tend to refinance concurrently, triggering what is known as a *refinancing* (or *prepayment*) wave. In fact, you might've contributed to the last refinancing wave that began in 2002 as rates dropped to historic lows. The last two reasons for prepays are home sales and defaults.

Unfortunately, what's good for homeowners is bad for investors because prepays rise when refinancing activity accelerates. And when prepays accelerate, the amount of principal you receive will be larger than expected. This is called *prepayment risk* (see Table 17.1).

But why is that a risk? After all, you're receiving principal earlier than you expected. Who in their right mind wouldn't want to be paid back sooner rather than later? Well, a bond investor, that's who, and for one simple reason—*reinvestment risk.* Remember our discussion earlier? It's the same predicament you face if any bond is called—principal is suddenly available just when yields on comparable securities are lower than the interest earned on the security that's being redeemed.

The early return of principal automatically reduces the size of the mortgage pool. Since the coupon rate is fixed, a smaller amount of principal generates less interest income, causing yields to decline. Remember, mortgage yields do not include principal even though it's

TABLE 17.1 Mortgage Prepayment Effects

Interest Rates		Refinancings		Prepayment Speeds		Average Life
Rise	→	Decline	→	Slower	→	Lengthens
Decline	→	Rise	→	Faster	→	Shortens

regularly part of monthly payments. After all, repaid principal is considered a return *of*—not *on*—your investment.

You may be wondering how a mortgage security can have a maturity date like other bonds if its underlying collateral can be repaid at any time. Good point. Truth is, even though the bond cannot extend beyond its stated maturity, for all intents and purposes, the specific date does not apply. That's right, just go ahead and ignore it, because if you want to be a mortgage investor, you're just going to have to settle for an estimate. I'm not kidding.

Lack of a defined maturity is unique to mortgage bonds. It's due to the unpredictable behavior of homeowners, which makes it impossible to assign hard-and-fast principal repayment dates. For that reason, the amount and speed of prepayments cannot be forecast with certainty either. That's why mortgage traders use historical data to predict the pace of prepayments, or *prepayment speeds.*

So, what's that got to do with maturities? Well, by estimating a prepayment speed, traders are able to assign each mortgage bond a *weighted average life,* or simply *average life.* Roughly put, average life is the estimated number of years it takes to return half a mortgage pool's principal to the investor. As with other bond maturities, the longer the average life, the more sensitive the price is to interest rate fluctuations. For instance, due to the popularity of 15- and 30-year conventional home loans, most mortgage bonds are issued with 15- and 30-year stated maturities. True, that's the underlying collateral, but mortgage investors will not have to wait that long for principal to be repaid. That's where average life comes in. Of course, since prepayments could suddenly accelerate or slow down, that estimated maturity is bound to change—if prepayments are faster than had been assumed, average life is going to shorten; if prepays are slower, average life would lengthen (see Table 17.1).

Be aware that assumptions about prepay speeds usually differ among bond traders. Most of them use the Public Securities Association (PSA) standard (also known as the prepayment speed assumption), which assumes new mortgage loans are less likely to be prepaid than older ones.

In order to determine how fast or slow PSA speeds should be, traders test mortgage bonds in empirical models to measure their performance under different interest rate scenarios. Prepay assumptions are critically important since they determine average life and, by extension, price and yield. Although increasingly sophisticated models are producing more accurate results, make sure you are aware of the trader's outlook since your bond's performance is going to depend on the accuracy of these assumptions.

We talked about what happens when interest rates drop, but what happens if they rise? Well, it's good news for long-term investors since prepayments would slow. The bad news, though, is that prepayments would slow. Huh? You read it right—if rates increased after you bought a mortgage bond, more principal would remain in the loan pool for a longer period of time. That means average life would lengthen and your money would likely be tied up longer than you may have anticipated. For example, a sudden upward move in interest rates could easily double a mortgage bond's average life. This is commonly known as *extension risk*.

There is one other feature that's important to consider when purchasing mortgage bonds—it's called *negative convexity* (see Figure 17.3).

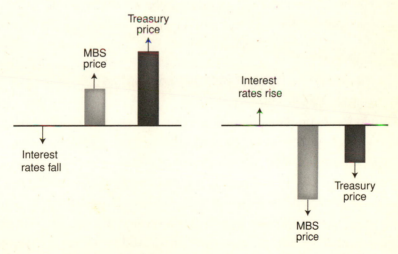

FIGURE 17.3   Negative Convexity

Since you asked, convexity is just the second derivative of a bond's price for given changes in yield. Got it? Well, don't worry about it, because for our bare essential purposes, what you need to know is pretty straightforward. Negative convexity just means that mortgage bond prices tend to decline more than other types of bonds when interest rates are rising. Conversely, they appreciate less when interest rates are falling. If you've already concluded that mortgage bond prices are more vulnerable to interest rate shifts than other types of fixed-income securities, you're right. Much like The Three Bears, (there they are again!) the MBS market likes its interest rates "just right."

That was a lot of information to absorb, so let's do a quick review of the key differences between mortgage bonds and other types of fixed-income securities:

- Cash flow consists of interest and principal and is paid monthly instead of semiannually.

- The nature of the underlying collateral causes the payment amount to vary.

- A fluctuating average life replaces final maturity date.

- Negative convexity causes prices to be more vulnerable to interest rate shifts than other types of bonds.

Types of Mortgage Securities

The two most common types of mortgage bonds purchased by individual investors are pass-throughs and *collateralized mortgage obligations*.

The majority of mortgage bonds are pass-through securities, or simply *pass-throughs*. Pass-throughs are merely conduits—mortgage payments are collected in a pool and distributed (or passed-through, get it?) to bond investors through a trust that's created at issuance. Although Fannie Mae and Freddie Mac issue approximately 75 percent of all pass-throughs, many investors favor Ginnie Mae because of its U.S. government guarantee (however, unlike other mortgage securities, these require a minimum initial investment of $25,000). Financial institutions also create *private label pass-throughs.* Although private label issuers are not agencies, these bonds are usually rated Triple-A or Double-A.

Cash flow could also be distributed according to a specific set of rules (rather than just passed on). These bonds are known as collateralized mortgage obligations, or CMOs (less commonly called *real estate mortgage investment conduits* or REMICs). CMOs are just a group of pass-through securities. As a result, a CMO issue is much larger than the average $20 million pass-through pool—it has recently ranged between $300 million to $500 million.

That's the easy part. The problem is that since these bonds contain different mortgage pools, the CMO structure is inordinately complex. And that's an understatement. Consequently, they're more volatile than pass-throughs. This is largely because CMO bonds are carved into different classes, or *tranches.* (I didn't study French either—tranche means "slice.") On average, CMOs contain 60 to 100 different tranches. Each tranche receives principal and interest according to a prescribed set of rules, such as an estimated *window* between the first and last principal payments. In the period prior to the first principal payment—known as the *lockout*—monthly cash flow consists of interest only. In effect, these features provide a way to customize a CMO's income stream.

Types of CMOs

Although there are nearly 40 different types of CMOs, most individual investors focus on two types: sequential bonds and planned amortization class (PAC) bonds. These are both known as *plain vanilla* CMOs. Fannie Mae, Freddie Mac, and—to a lesser degree—Ginnie Mae account for approximately two-thirds of all CMO issuance.

A *sequential bond* is fairly straightforward. In its simplest form, it could have four separate tranches labeled A, B, C, and D. The first tranche absorbs prepayment cash flow, or principal, first. When that's paid off, the next tranche begins, followed by each tranche in succession. Since the principal of each tranche is paid off sequentially, the average life of A is shorter than B, B is shorter than C, and C is shorter than D.

Additionally, sequential structures could also have a non-interest-paying Z-tranche. Z-bonds typically have the longest average lives—usually beyond 20 years—so they also offer the highest yields. Since they are structured as zero coupon securities, interest is not received by the investor. Instead, it accrues to face value and when the lockout period ends, principal and interest are repaid.

The amount of time between each sequential tranche varies depending on prepayment speeds. For example, the first tranche might be paid off in 3 to 5 years, the second in 7 to 10 years, and the third in 12 to 15 years. You get the idea.

Tranches in *PAC bond* structures behave differently than those in sequentials. The cash flow allocated to each tranche is distributed based on a schedule. This schedule has certain preset limits for prepayment amounts, so average life and yield are relatively stable. PACs are able to remain within these prescribed limits due to a special companion tranche containing *support bonds.* Support bonds absorb prepayments from PAC tranches and compensate the PAC bond for any shortfall in principal payments. Although supports offer more yield than other tranches, there's a reason—they're highly volatile and more sensitive to interest rates. As a result, they're also subject to more reinvestment and extension risk than other mortgage bonds. So be extra cautious with these securities, especially if you're faced with rapidly changing market conditions.

CMOs are also issued as *whole loans.* Whole loans are nonagency CMOs, which means they're created by financial institutions in the private sector—such as investment banks—and are the sole obligation of those issuers. These CMOs compensate for the lack of a direct or implicit U.S. government guarantee by offering investors slightly more yield. Whole loans have two different debt classes—senior and junior. Most whole loans are issued as senior debt and are rated Triple-A because of their strong collateral. Junior subordinated issues are usually rated Double-A or Single-A since they absorb loan defaults before the senior debt is affected.

CMOs have the most complex structures in the bond market, so don't be discouraged if you're a little confused. Believe it or not, we didn't even review most of the different types—with obscure monikers such as IO, PO, inverse floater, and "busted PAC." But there's a good reason for these omissions—most CMO structures are not commonly offered to individual investors. Whether you invest in CMOs or pass-throughs, just keep in mind that cash flow fluctuates and principal is not repaid on a specific date. Most importantly, develop a firm understanding of these securities *before* you invest. One of the cardinal rules come to mind: *Don't buy what you don't understand.*

Asset-Backed Securities

I decided to forgo a separate section on asset-backed securities (ABSs) since, like many CMOs, they're not typically offered to individual investors. This is due to a variety of uninteresting reasons commonly associated with regulatory hurdles that make it difficult for individuals to participate. But since the ABS sector represents a growing part of the fixed-income market, it deserves mention.

ABSs are securitized and structured much like mortgages, except they're backed by receivables from assets other than real estate—such as credit card loans, airplane leases, and auto loans. A number of more creative structures have also been issued. Perhaps the most famous was the $55 million bond issue launched in 1997 against royalty payments earned by David Bowie—an aging rock star for those of you assuming he invented a knife. Even James Brown—that's right, the Godfather of Soul himself—issued asset-backed securities against future royalties. Although securities collateralized by music royalties are mildly interesting, they're also pretty atypical—just chalk it up to the go-go '90s, when anything was possible.

chapter eighteen
CORPORATE BONDS

The Bare Essentials

❦ The corporate bond market is normally segregated into four industry sectors: *finance, industrials, transportation,* and *utilities.*

❦ The *capital structure* ranks bonds according to the claim they have on a company's assets.

❦ Since all corporate issuers carry some degree of risk, credit ratings are critical. These are divided into two categories: *investment-grade* (or *high-grade*) and *high-yield* (or *junk)* bonds.

❦ Credit ratings are not stagnant. *Upgrades* occur when financial security strengthens, while *downgrades* occur when it deteriorates. These ratings changes impact investors and issuers alike.

Most large companies that issue stock also issue *corporate bonds,* or just plain *corporates.* As we mentioned earlier, proceeds from these debt sales are used for a variety of purposes, such as working capital, building factories, or acquiring other companies. Companies have even issued bonds to buy back common stock.

The corporate bond market is normally segregated into four industry sectors: *finance*, which includes banks, broker-dealers, and insurance companies; *industrials*, such as manufacturing and energy companies;

transportation, such as railroads and airlines; and *utilities*, which are principally electric, gas, and telecommunication providers.

Unlike common stock, corporate bonds are not homogenous. That's because corporations have a *capital structure*, which ranks bonds according to the claim they have on a company's assets. The capital structure in Table 18.1 could be further divided into even more tiers, but for our bare essential purposes, this level of detail is sufficient.

Notice how debt ranks higher than equity, and how common stock is dead last. That's because equity investors are owners, not creditors, and have last dibs on the assets should a company default. You can see that senior secured bonds are, well, the most secure. That's because specific assets collateralize them. Secured bonds include *equipment trust certificates* (transportation equipment), *first mortgage bonds* (real estate), and *collateral trust bonds* (financial assets).

Any bonds that are not secured are known collectively as *debentures*. In effect, these bonds are backed by an issuer's general credit standing rather than by specific assets. Most corporates are issued as debentures, and most debentures are issued as senior unsecured debt.

Corporate bonds are issued at par with maturities from 2 to 30 years. Although there are putable, floating-rate, and step-up note structures, most corporates are bullets or straight callables. Large corporations also issue short-term debt, known as *commercial paper* (CP), which matures

TABLE 18.1 Corporate Capital Structure

Type of Debt	*Classification*	*Ranking*
Collateralized debt	Senior secured	*Highest*
Unsecured debt (debentures)	Senior unsecured Senior subordinated Subordinated Junior subordinated	
Equity	Preferred stock Common stock	*Lowest*

in 270 days or less. However, since individual investors rarely purchase these securities directly, we'll discuss them briefly in Chapter 26.

Medium-Term Notes

Medium-term notes, or MTNs, are considered senior unsecured debt, but differ from other corporate bonds in several fundamental ways. For instance, most corporates pay interest semiannually, yet MTNs also can generate quarterly or monthly payments. Although maturities range from 9 months to 40 years, most MTNs are structured as bullets in the 2- to 5-year range, and as 10- and 15-year callable securities.

Most MTNs retain a unique put feature known as the *survivor's option*—affectionately known as the *death put*—which allows heirs to redeem bonds at par should the registered owner of the security die, even if it's trading at a steep discount (most have a holding period of 6 to 12 months). As morbid as the survivor's option sounds, it is useful for estate planning purposes. MTNs may remind some of you of its predecessor—U.S. Treasury "flower bonds," which were initially issued to help investors pay inheritance taxes.

Medium-term note issuance size is much smaller than other senior debt issues since these are retail bond offerings. These are also considered *shelf offerings*, which means a company may register them up to two years in advance and issue bonds whenever funds are needed or market conditions are favorable. As a result, MTNs are continuously issued, sometimes weekly, and do not trade actively in the secondary market. In other words, they're fairly illiquid compared to other corporate bonds (do you recall our discussion about liquidity?). So if you purchase an MTN, be prepared to hold it until maturity.

Credit Quality

Corporate bonds yield more than Treasury and agency securities since all issuers carry some degree of risk. Additionally, since no two balance sheets are created equal, corporates should be thoroughly evaluated before you invest. As we briefly discussed earlier, Moody's, S&P, and Fitch provide ratings that allow us to quickly assess a company's credit quality.

Credit ratings are the most important determinant of corporate bond yields. For that reason, ratings have a tremendous impact on a company's cost of capital. Many factors are evaluated, such as the quality of an issuer's balance sheet and the depth of its current management team. External factors are considered as well, such as market share, industry trends, and competition. Credit ratings are organized on a scale that's divided into two distinct categories: *investment-grade* and *high-yield*.

Investment-Grade Bonds

Investment-grade (also known as *high-grade*) bonds comprise issuers that are deemed to be in good financial health and are unlikely to have trouble meeting their debt obligations. Bonds are ranked from Triple-A (highest) to Triple-B (lowest). Except for Triple-A, each ratings category is further divided into three different levels. These levels are known as *notches,* as in, "That bond is only two notches from Triple-A" (see Table 18.2).

You probably noticed that Moody's ratings are slightly different from S&P and Fitch. That's because Moody's is managed by an aging rock group that still strives to be different. Just checking to make sure you're awake. Despite Moody's eccentric system, it's safe to assume that rankings from all three agencies are comparable and quantified with similar standards.

When you request a corporate bond rating, it's commonly understood that Moody's is quoted first. Consequently, Moody's appears on the left, S&P on the right, and Fitch is ignored. This time I'm not kidding. Don't get me wrong—Fitch follows the same rigorous methodology as its peers. So it's not a judgment call on my part, it's just the way things are. For example, you'll see corporate bond ratings written as follows: Aa2/AA. Unless otherwise stated, the second rating is always S&P. Since each agency employs its own set of analysts, don't be surprised

TABLE 18.2 Investment-Grade Credit Ratings

Moody's	*S&P*	*Fitch*	*Also known as . . .*	*Risk characteristics*
Aaa	AAA	AAA	Triple-A	Exceptional financial security; smallest degree of risk
Aa1	AA+	AA+	High Double-A	Excellent financial security;
Aa2	AA	AA	Mid Double-A	long-term risks slightly
Aa3	AA−	AA−	Low Double-A	larger than Triple-A
A1	A+	A+	High Single-A	Good financial security;
A2	A	A	Mid Single-A	susceptible to credit
A3	A−	A−	Low Single-A	quality impairment
Baa1	BBB+	BBB+	High Triple-B	Adequate financial security;
Baa2	BBB	BBB	Mid Triple-B	ability to sustain investment-
Baa3	BBB−	BBB−	Low Triple-B	grade credit status over the long term uncertain

when—not if—different ratings are assigned to the same issue. For example, a bond could be rated Baa1 by Moody's and A− by S&P (Baa1/A−). This *split rating* sometimes occurs when a company is undergoing a significant transition—such as a senior management shakeup—and the rating agencies disagree about the nature or timing of its outcome. However, the difference rarely exceeds more than one or two notches.

Now let's go back to the capital structure (see Table 18.1). Since some debt is more senior than others, the ratings agencies assign different ratings depending on rank. For example, senior unsecured debt could be rated Low Double-A, senior subordinated High Single-A, and junior subordinated Mid Single-A. In practice, senior unsecured debt ratings are typically used when discussing corporate credit quality.

You might be wondering if securities other than corporate bonds also receive credit ratings. And even if you're not wondering, I'm going to tell you anyway. Treasuries are not rated since there's no risk to assess—they're issued by a Washington, D.C. enterprise that prints its own currency.

Agency bonds are Triple-A, but their subordinated debt (which is issued less frequently) is rated Double-A. Most mortgage securities are considered Triple-A due to their affiliation with government agencies and the strength of their underlying collateral. Several other types of securities are also rated, and we'll discuss them in upcoming chapters.

High-Yield Bonds

Companies that do not receive investment-grade ratings are considered *high-yield*. Although high-yield issuers have become more prominent participants in the corporate bond market, they remain a small percentage of its overall size. High-yield companies are a cross section of healthy start-ups, struggling businesses, and established, but highly leveraged, issuers. The speculative quality of these bonds earned them the "junk bond," name, though issuers prefer the less derogatory "high-yield." The ratings agencies rank these bonds from Ba1 to C (Moody's), and from "BB+" to "D" (S&P and Fitch) (see Table 18.3).

High-yield issuance gathered momentum in the 1980s and was primarily used for hostile takeovers and leveraged buyouts. Throughout this period, high-yield debt securities were known as junk bonds, and still are in many circles. The label "junk" refers to their less certain

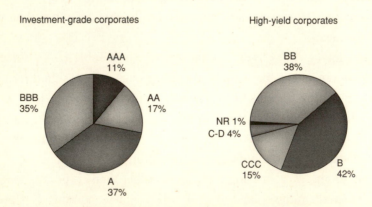

Source: Lehman Brothers, approximations as of June 2003.

FIGURE 18.1 Corporate Bond Market by Credit Rating

Table 18.3 High-Yield Credit Ratings

Moody's	S&P	Fitch	Also known as . . .	Risk characteristics
Ba1	BB+	BB+	High Double-B	Questionable financial secuity;
Ba2	BB	BB	Mid Double-B	ability to meet debt
Ba3	BB–	BB–	Low Double-B	obligations is uncertain
B1	B+	B+	High Single-B	Poor financial security; low
B2	B	B	Mid Single-B	probability of fulfilling
B3	B–	B–	Low Single-B	debt obligations
Caa1	CCC+	CCC+	High Triple-C	Very poor financial security;
Caa2	CCC	CCC	Mid Triple-C	could be verging on or in
Caa3	CCC–	CCC–	Low Triple-C	default
Ca1	CC+	CC+	High Double-C	Extremely poor financial
Ca2	CC	CC	Mid Double-C	security; often in default
Ca3	CC–	CC–	Low Double-C	
C	C+	C+	High Single-C	Lowest rated; usually in
	C	C	Mid Single-C	default with low potential
	C–	C–	Low Single-C	recovery value
No rating	D	D	Default	Default

credit quality, since a highly-leveraged company has less margin for error to meet its obligations than, say, a more stable corporate borrower or government. Today, this market functions much like the investment-grade sector, providing capital to many mainstream companies. However, the longest maturity offered by high-yield issuers is usually 10 years, as opposed to conventional 30-year maturities offered by investment-grade issuers.

"High-yield" is an accurate description since, after all, bond yields should rise as credit quality descends. In fact, these bonds generally provide investors with as much as 150 to 500 basis points more than investment-grade corporate yields. Most high-yield bonds also include special covenants to protect investors. The most common feature is the *poison put,* which allows bonds to be redeemed at a slight premium if there's a change of control, such as a company buyout.

Many high-yield bonds are not available to individual investors. These bonds are known as *private placements* since they're sold directly to institutional investors rather than through a public offering. (Investment-grade private placements also are issued, but it's far less common than in the high-yield sector.) Although these issues are not public offerings, they're still subject to an SEC regulation known as Rule 144A. This rule requires private placements only be sold to qualified institutional buyers (QIBs). Essentially, it's another reason why it's more appropriate for individuals to participate in this market through mutual funds, especially if you have less than $100,000 targeted for high-yield bonds.

Leverage and Default

One way to quickly gauge leverage is to use a simple ratio that compares total debt to cash flow. For example, if a company had $500 million in debt and $100 million in cash flow, it would be "5-times leveraged." If cash flow is $50 million, then it's trading at "10-times leverage." You get the idea—higher numbers imply more risk. However, be aware that this ratio is useless unless it's placed in its proper context. This is because some industries are naturally more leveraged than others. As a rule, the more stable an industry's cash flows, the more leverage it can tolerate.

Non-investment-grade companies carry considerable leverage—that's when their debt is considered too high relative to their current cash flow or total capital. Translation: There's a heightened risk of default. In fact, the default rate among high-yield corporate issuers peaked at an extraordinary 12.8 percent in 2002, eclipsing the prior 10.3 percent record set in 1991.

Defaulted issuers typically attempt to reorganize under Chapter 11 bankruptcy law. Although interest payments have been halted, defaulted bonds could still have *recovery value.* Historically, recovery values have averaged 50 cents on the dollar, although this estimate has declined in recent years. Bear in mind that bond investors quite often end up with a combination of cash and new securities if the issuer emerges from Chapter 11. But, hey, stock investors usually get nothing. That's the benefit of being a creditor. The bad news is that you could be waiting many, many moons for the defaulted company to reemerge from Chapter 11 in order to stake your claim. For that reason, most individual bondholders usually are better off liquidating these bonds in the *distressed market,* where professional "vulture" investors place bets among the carnage of troubled or defaulted issuers.

Upgrades and Downgrades

Credit agencies closely monitor the developments of rated issuers. Any material change to a company's financial status could impact its credit rating. When this occurs, it's called a *ratings action,* or more specifically an *upgrade* or a *downgrade.*

As the names imply, an upgrade occurs when the issuer's financial profile strengthens and a downgrade is triggered when its credit quality deteriorates. For example, if an acquisition bolsters a Single-A company's balance sheet without adding additional debt, it could be rewarded with an upgrade to Double-A. However, if the acquisition significantly enlarges debt relative to earnings, the issuer just as easily could be downgraded to Triple-B. By the way, any company that gets downgraded from Triple-B to Double-B (in other words, from investment-grade to high-yield) is a *fallen angel.* Just like Lucifer. So don't even think for a minute that the bond market is a godless enterprise.

Moody's and S&P provide clues to their intermediate and long-term views by assigning a *Positive, Negative, Stable,* or *Developing Outlook.* When agencies want to communicate possible short-term ratings actions, an issuer is placed *Under Review* at Moody's or on *CreditWatch* at S&P. A positive or negative bias indicates whether an upgrade or downgrade is being considered. Just like the ratings themselves, agency opinions can differ here as well. But it's pretty uncommon for the same issuer to have a positive bias at one agency and a negative bias at another. These designations, by the way, are not necessarily a precursor to actual ratings actions.

Upgrades and Downgrades: An Issuers Viewpoint

Although credit ratings are a critical tool for bond investors, they're no less important for issuers—albeit for an entirely different reason. Think about it—if the market demands a higher yield from a lower-rated issuer than from a higher-rated issuer, a rating change could have a significant impact on a company's total borrowing costs and its ability to readily access the capital markets. In other words, higher credit ratings reduce total interest expense.

For instance, suppose two Single-A industrial companies issued 10-year bonds with a 7 percent coupon in January. In June, the rating agencies upgraded one of these companies to Low Double-A. If both companies launched another 10-year deal in December, what do you think would occur? That's right, the Double-A bonds would be offered with a lower coupon to reflect their lower degree of risk.

Let's take it one step further. If the Single-A rated company has to pay 7 percent to launch a $300 million issue of 10-year bonds, annual interest expense would be $21 million ($300 million × 7 percent). The upgraded Double-A issuer could raise that amount of capital by compensating investors with, say, a 6.8 percent coupon. As a result, the Double-A company's borrowing costs drop to $20.4 million ($300 million × 6.8 percent), amounting to an annual savings of $600,000. Now you can imagine how ratings impact large issuers.

chapter nineteen
MUNICIPAL BONDS

The Bare Essentials

- State and local governments issue *municipal bonds* to finance projects that serve the public interest. *General obligation* (*GO*s) and *revenue bonds* are the two main types.

- Municipals are popular with individual investors since they can provide tax-free interest income.

- Municipalities are assigned credit ratings just like corporate issuers. They may also purchase insurance to ensure that a new bond issue receives a Triple-A rating.

- Since municipals are tax-advantaged, they have lower nominal yields than their taxable fixed-income counterparts. *Taxable equivalent yields* should be calculated to fairly compare municipal and taxable yields.

On the way home from work, you noticed that two lanes are being added to accommodate increased traffic caused by the residents of a new housing development. The hospital finally broke ground for its new emergency wing, and another high school is being built. Did you ever wonder who's footing the bill for all these projects?

I know what you're thinking—we are. That's why we pay taxes. In reality, though, that's only partially correct, because—brace yourself—

politicians overspend their budgets. As a result, states, cities, counties, and towns issue *municipal bonds* to help finance public works projects. In fact, according to the Bond Market Association, approximately 50,000 issuers are responsible for the nearly $2 trillion of municipal debt currently outstanding. These bonds are more commonly known as *municipals,* or—if you really want to be cool—*munis.* Most municipal bond maturities range from 2 to 30 years and pay semiannual interest. Par value is $1,000, yet they are commonly sold in minimum increments of $5,000. Although these bonds are sensitive to interest rate fluctuations, supply and demand have a greater impact on municipals than on most other fixed-income sectors.

Municipal bonds are especially popular with U.S. investors because the federal government does not tax interest generated by the majority of these bonds. Additionally, most state and local municipalities allow investors to enjoy tax-free income from the securities issued by their home states. Bonds issued by U.S. territories—such as Puerto Rico, Guam, and the U.S. Virgin Islands—are tax-exempt for residents of all states. Although residents of seven states do not have to pay state income tax, municipal bonds provide a real benefit for the rest of us who do.

In fact, municipal securities are the only type of bond that have the potential to generate fully tax-free income (although Treasuries and a few agency issuers provide some tax relief, federal income tax must be paid). For that reason, individuals purchase more municipals than any other bonds. In fact, the muni market is the only major bond sector that's not dominated by institutional investors. There are exceptions to municipal bond tax exemptions (you're surprised?), so be sure to check with a tax advisor before purchasing these securities. It's also important to keep in mind that regardless of your status, capital gains on municipal bonds are subject to federal taxes.

Categories of Municipal Bonds

Most municipal bonds fall into one of three categories: public purpose, nongovernmental purpose, and private activity bonds. Although you'd

get a blank stare if you asked your financial advisor for a nongovernmental purpose bond, it helps to understand the differences when evaluating whether or not these bonds are appropriate for your portfolio:

Public purpose bonds are issued directly by state or local authorities for
the types of projects you'd expect governments to finance. This includes
construction of public schools, sanitation facilities, water treatment plants,
and highways. These bonds are exempt from federal, state and local taxes.

Nongovernmental purpose bonds are also fully tax-exempt securities.
These bonds are used to fund initiatives that more narrowly serve the
public interest or are associated with the private sector, for example,
transportation authorities, private hospitals, and universities.

Private activity bonds are issued by municipalities but are associated with
projects that are not government-run. These issues may be taxable, depending on the extent to which they benefit the public interest and typically include bonds that finance student loans, airports, industrial developments, or
other special projects. For example, let's say your state has successfully
recruited a professional baseball team. In order to attract the franchise, local
politicians promised the team a new stadium would be built. However, the
stadium is slated to cost approximately $300 million. Since government cof-
fers aren't routinely overflowing with cash, municipal bonds are issued to
support the project. The long-term objective here is to help boost local businesses and, in turn, increase tax revenue.

Private activity bonds also qualify as alternative minimum tax (AMT)
issues. The AMT rule was created by the IRS to ensure that wealthy investors at least pay some taxes regardless of the amount of deductions or
exemptions. If you suspect you might fit the profile, make sure you
check with a tax accountant *before* you invest. Otherwise, you might
purchase an AMT bond expecting to generate tax-exempt income but
instead be required to pay taxes on the interest.

General Obligation and Revenue Bonds

The two most common types of municipal securities are *general obligation* (GO) bonds and *Revenue* bonds. Municipalities that have the ability

to tax constituents issue GOs. State governments dominate this type of issuance, followed by cities with large public infrastructures, such as New York and Chicago. Revenue bonds, on the other hand, are backed by revenue and fees collected by the facility that's being funded. For example, a highway, bridge, or tunnel could support interest payments with revenue from tolls, and airport bonds would generate revenue by leasing commercial space and charging landing fees.

GOs typically have better credit quality and experience higher demand than revenue bonds since issuers can raise taxes or tap myriad revenue streams to meet interest payments if necessary. A revenue bond is not as secure since debt service is directly supported by income generated by a specific project.

Municipalities also issue taxable bonds, though it only represents a small part of the municipal market. Taxables are issued when the federal government is unwilling to sanction certain projects that do not broadly serve the public interest. These bonds include corporate-backed municipal debt related to pollution control or waste disposal. These also are issued when a municipality exceeds its tax-exempt issuance limit for certain types of bonds. Taxable munis offer yields comparable to similarly rated corporate securities.

Short-Term Notes

Anticipation notes, which are used to bridge financing gaps until future revenue is received, are short-term issues—they are the municipal market's version of corporate commercial paper. And, just like their corporate counterparts, these bonds are rated on a different scale than longer-term municipal securities (see Table 19.1).

Most of these notes are issued at par and pay interest at maturity. Although most mature in less than one year, they are also issued for 18 months—investors receive an interim interest payment before maturity. Municipalities usually try to avoid issuing these notes beyond 18 months because they could become taxable. The most commonly issued antici-

TABLE 19.1 Municipal Short-Term Ratings

Moody's	S&P	Risk Characteristics
MIG 1/VMIG 1	SP-1+	Superior quality
MIG 2/VMIG 2	SP-1	High quality
MIG 3/VMIG 3	SP-2	Good quality
SG	SP-3	Speculative quality

pation notes include *tax anticipation notes* (TANs), *revenue anticipation notes* (RANs), *tax and revenue anticipation notes* (TRANs), and *bond anticipation notes* (BANs).

Another type of short-term municipal is the *variable-rate demand note,* commonly known as a *floating-rate note,* or *floater.* These are appropriate for very short-term investment needs since they're issued with 7-day and 28-day maturities. You could roll your principal into the same maturity each time it comes due, but the fixed rate will be *reset* to reflect supply and demand.

Structure

Municipals are issued as term and serial bonds. These are noncallable, or have early redemption features, such as put or call provisions. Callable bonds usually have at least 10 years of call protection. Zero coupon munis are also issued with maturities up to 40 years, providing investors with flexibility for specific long-term savings objectives (the "phantom" income would be tax-free). And, just like the corporate sector, municipalities can issue sinking fund bonds.

Sometimes callable munis are *pre-refunded. Pre-re*'s are simply callable bonds that have been refinanced. Here's how it works: When interest rates fall, issuers want to lock in lower borrowing costs, just like you might refinance a mortgage. But if a bond still has call protection, it cannot be retired. To circumvent this, municipalities get a little creative.

They issue a *refunding bond* at a lower interest rate and purchase Treasuries with the proceeds. In exchange, bondholders receive a municipal bond collateralized by U.S. Treasury securities. Treasuries pay interest on these bonds until the first call date. At that time, the muni is redeemed and Treasuries are sold to repay principal. This process is also applied to noncallable bonds, but that's called *escrowed to maturity*.

Credit Quality

Municipalities are assigned credit ratings by at least two of the three major agencies on the same scale we discussed in the previous chapter (Tables 18.2 and 18.3). Although quality varies, most municipals are rated investment-grade. Additionally, defaults in this market are rare. According to a recent study by S&P, the long-term historical default rate for investment-grade municipal bonds is less than 1.0 percent.

Ratings agencies use different criteria to assess municipalities as opposed to corporate entities. For instance, profitability and market share are important when evaluating a corporate issuer. On the other hand, growth of tax receipts and stability of cash flow to expenses are critical credit quality considerations for GOs and revenue bonds, respectively.

Insured Bonds

One of the advantages of the municipal market is insurance. That's right, just like you buy car insurance, municipal issuers commonly purchase insurance for their bonds. Insurance guarantees investors that all interest and principal will be paid should the issuer default. In effect, the issuer is taking out a life insurance policy on itself. The lower its underlying credit quality, the more it will have to pay for the coverage. Some taxable issuers, such as Canadian provinces and energy companies, have also insured bond issues. But among non-municipal issuers, that's the exception, not the rule.

The major bond insurers, which are Triple-A rated, include AMBAC (American Municipal Bond Assurance Company), FGIC (Financial Guarantee Insurance Company), FSA (Financial Security Assurance), and MBIA (Municipal Bond Insurance Association). You'll see these acronyms attached to the description of insured offerings. You'll also hear them commonly marketed this way, as in, "the bond is AMBAC-insured."

Credit agencies automatically bestow Triple-A ratings on insured municipal bonds. In other words, regardless of underlying credit quality, an insured bond offers you the highest credit safety. This can be a great comfort, especially since insurance provides coverage for the life of the security. In fact, since the muni market typically attracts conservative investors, demand for insured bonds has grown exponentially. Today, nearly one out of every two new municipal offerings is insured.

Let's look at an example. Suppose two municipalities were about to issue bonds—one is rated High Single-A, and the other is rated Low Triple-B. On a stand-alone basis, the difference in yield could be substantial because of credit risk. But if each issuer bought municipal insurance, they'd level the playing field (see Figure 19.1). Then the spread would significantly narrow as both yields declined—particularly the Triple-B. To be sure, there are other factors that affect price and yield, but when you remove credit quality concerns, you substantially reduce risk.

In most cases, municipalities can buy insurance when they issue new securities. However, insurers typically restrict the amount of insurance they're willing to extend. For that reason, municipalities can be prevented from buying insurance if their limit is reached. Additionally, insurance only applies to a particular bond issue, not to the issuer's

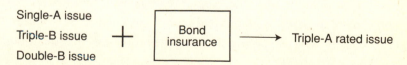

FIGURE 19.1 **Effect of Municipal Bond Insurance on Credit Ratings**

underlying credit rating. So don't be surprised to see two bonds from the same issuer with different ratings—one reflecting its underlying credit quality and the other insured Triple-A. And, since even the lowest-rated issuers could purchase insurance, a junk-rated issue could be Triple-A! Who said if you put lipstick on a pig, it's still a pig?

However, insurers do discriminate. Just like life insurance companies, they cautiously evaluate the health of potential customers before providing coverage. The bond market discriminates as well. For instance, munis that are Triple-A rated without insurance typically yield less than insured bond issues. Additionally, an insured Triple-A revenue bond would trade cheaper than an insured GO. You get the idea. These incremental differences in yield, however, are usually no more than 20 to 30 basis points.

Municipal insurance has been a boon for both investors and issuers. These bonds enjoy strong demand because investors are reassured by the Triple-A guarantee. Meanwhile, issuers are happy to accommodate the demand because—despite the cost of insurance—it enables them to lower borrowing costs.

Taxable Equivalent Yield

Let's compare two 10-year Single-A securities: one is a 6.5 percent municipal bond, and the other is a 6.5 percent corporate bond. Which would be a better value for an investor in the 33 percent federal tax bracket? The municipal bond, of course, since interest would be tax-exempt. However, this kind of comparison is rare since municipals offer lower nominal yields due to their tax-advantaged status. That's also why comparing tax-free municipal yields to taxable bond yields is not an accurate way to assess value. Apples to oranges, if you will. As a result, you'll need to adjust a muni yield in order to fairly compare it to a taxable security. You can do this by using the following equation for taxable equivalent yield (TEY):

$$\text{Taxable equivalent yield} = \frac{\text{municipal YTM}}{(1 - \text{your marginal income tax rate})}$$

where YTM is yield to maturity and your marginal income tax rate is the sum of your federal, state, and local taxes.

Be aware that TEY doesn't account for differences in maturity or credit quality. For example, would it be fair to compare the TEY of a 10-year Triple-B muni to a 10-year Double-A corporate bond? How about a 30-year MBIA-insured municipal bond to a 2-year agency? You get the point.

Let's plug these variables into the TEY formula to determine whether a 15-year Single-A municipal bond at 5 percent YTM offers a better yield than a 15-year Single-A corporate bond with a 7.5 percent YTM. Let's assume 33 percent federal and 4 percent state tax:

$$\text{Taxable equivalent yield} = \frac{\text{municipal YTM}}{(1 - \text{your marginal income tax rate})}$$

$$= \frac{5.0\%}{(1 - 0.37)}$$

$$= \frac{0.05}{0.63}$$

$$= 0.079 = 7.9\%$$

Since TEY equals 7.9 percent, the 5.0 percent municipal bond would provide a higher rate of return than the 7.5 percent corporate issue. But which one would be better for your IRA? Here's a hint: You don't pay taxes on interest generated in an IRA. *That's why municipal bonds do not belong in a tax-deferred account.* After all, why pick the lower yield if there's no tax benefit?

As you probably surmised, the more income tax you pay, the more beneficial a muni bond becomes. In fact, these bonds generally provide investors in the 28% bracket and above with a higher *after tax* yield than

TABLE 19.2 Taxable Equivalent Yield

Tax-Exempt Yield	25% Federal + 4% State	28% Federal + 4% State	33% Federal + 4% State	35% Federal + 4% State
4.5%	6.34	6.62	7.14	7.38
5.0%	7.04	7.35	7.94	8.20
5.5%	7.75	8.09	8.73	9.02
6.0%	8.45	8.82	9.52	9.84

comparable taxable securities. Table 19.2 shows some examples of TEY for various income tax brackets.

You could bypass the math and just go to the Bond Market Association website (www.investinginbonds.com). There you'll find an easy-to-use *Tax-Free vs. Taxable Yield Comparison Calculator* that will calculate the taxable bond yield you will need in order to match the tax-exempt income generated by a municipal security.

By the way, if you live in a state with a low tax rate, you should consider out-of-state issues since yields could be competitive even without the in-state exemption. This is especially worthwhile when in-state yields are artificially low because of strong demand or a shortage of new supply. To determine whether an out-of-state bond provides better value than in-state securities, just subtract the state tax from 100 percent and multiply the out-of-state yield by that amount. Of course, residents in high-tax states (such as New York) may have difficulty finding these kinds of opportunities since more yield is needed to compensate for losing the in-state exemption.

Comparing Municipals to Treasuries

The TEY calculation might be useful when comparing munis to taxable bonds, but what about Treasury yields? After all, since they're exempt from state and local taxes, the TEY wouldn't apply. Well, kind of—you

still have to do the TEY calculation for your municipal bond, but you
also need to do one for your Treasury. Here's how to do it:

$$TEY = \frac{\text{Treasury YTM}}{(1 - \text{state and/or local income tax rate})}$$

By eliminating state and/or local taxes, the two taxable equivalent
yields are on equal footing. For example, if we're comparing a Triple-A
municipal bond with a 4.5 percent YTM to a Treasury bond with a 5 percent YTM, we calculate two taxable equivalent yields. Let's also assume
that these bonds have the same maturity, and the investor has a 33 percent federal and 4 percent combined state and local rate.

$$TEY = \frac{\text{municipal YTM}}{(1 - \text{your marginal income tax rate})}$$

$$= \frac{4.5\%}{(1 - 0.37)}$$

$$= \frac{0.045}{0.63}$$

$$= 0.071 = 7.1\%$$

$$TEY = \frac{\text{Treasury YTM}}{(1 - \text{state/local tax rate})}$$

$$= \frac{5.0\%}{(1 - 0.37)}$$

$$= \frac{0.05}{0.63}$$

$$= 0.079 = 7.9\%$$

On a taxable equivalent yield basis, the Treasury security provides
better value than the municipal bond.

Treasuries are commonly used by municipal bond analysts to express value. They do this by expressing municipal yields as a percentage of Treasury yields. For example, suppose 10-year Triple-A muni bonds yield 4.8 percent and 10-year Treasury notes yield 5.0 percent. Municipals would then be trading at 96 percent (divide 4.8 by 5) of Treasuries—meaning their yields capture 96 percent of Treasury yields. Since 80 percent is the 10-year historical average, these bonds present compelling value.

Remember, if bonds are being considered for a taxable account, you'd be doing yourself a disservice by overlooking the municipal sector. After all, as my accountant says, *it's not what you earn that matters most, it's what you keep after taxes.*

chapter twenty

INTERNATIONAL BONDS

The Bare Essentials

- Most fixed-income securities issued by foreign entities are structured similarly to U.S. debt. However, bonds issued in Europe pay interest annually, rather than semiannually.

- You could participate in the international market through U.S. dollar-denominated or local currency debt.

- U.S. dollar–denominated securities issued by non–U.S. entities are known as *Yankee* bonds.

- International bonds expose investors to myriad country-based uncertainties, collectively known as *sovereign risk*, and to *currency risk*.

Since the Soviet Union was dismantled—and the impact of its communist legacy diminished—more countries have jumped on the capital markets bandwagon than ever before. This has accelerated the growth of new stock exchanges and bond markets around the world and fostered a significant increase in cross-border investment flows. Even China, one of the last bastions of communism, is struggling to balance its seemingly contrary objectives of centralized planning and capitalist ideals. And despite some unforeseen turmoil along the way (Russia, after all, defaulted in 1998 and Argentina followed suit in 2001), the worldwide capital markets continue to grow exponentially.

Most sovereign nations have issued their own government bonds locally for some time—the counterparts to U.S. Treasuries, if you will. But private sector debt issuance has recently begun to outpace the volume of government issuance in some parts of the world. This is due largely to the privatization of formerly state-run industries, which has fueled demand for new investment capital.

In the past it was easy for U.S. bond investors to ignore overseas markets simply because of the breadth of domestic choices. But that view has become increasingly outdated as global business relationships become more intertwined. Moreover, as the delivery of real-time information has accelerated to lightning speed, U.S. market performance is more closely correlated to events outside its borders than ever before.

Even if you're a flag-waving patriot who "only invests in America," I've got a surprise for you—you're probably not. That's because most major corporations are earning a greater portion of their revenues from a fast-growing base of overseas customers. The increasing number of cross-border mergers and acquisitions has accelerated this trend. One day you may own bonds of a "solid American company" that suddenly transforms into a foreign-owned entity. That's exactly what happened to Chrysler bondholders when Germany-based Daimler Benz acquired that quintessential American industrial giant back in 1998.

Xenophobes should skip to the next chapter. But for the rest of us, these global developments are especially positive since they have generated a wider range of investment choices.

Most foreign-issued fixed-income securities—whether corporate or government—are structured similarly to U.S. bonds. However, bonds in Europe pay interest annually, rather than semiannually, including U.S. corporate securities issued there. Bonds that are issued in multiple European countries by U.S. (or non–European) issuers are often called *eurobonds*. Eurobonds that are denominated in U.S. dollars are—you guessed it—*eurodollar bonds*.

Sovereign Risk

International bonds have varying degrees of risk. Fortunately, the same rating agencies that evaluate U.S. companies provide ratings for bonds issued by foreign corporations and sovereign nations, which certainly alleviates much of the guesswork related to credit quality. Bondholders, though, are still vulnerable to myriad uncertainties naturally associated with investing in another country. Collectively, this is known as *sovereign risk*. Sovereign risk is related to event risk, though in this context it includes potential political or economic upheavals that could directly affect the performance of your investment. In the U.S. debt market, bonds issued by foreign governments are known as *sovereigns*.

Without a doubt, some countries have higher sovereign risk than others. Bonds issued by Great Britain, for instance, pose little sovereign risk to U.S. investors. But how about a country with a deeply corrupt political infrastructure and a leading presidential candidate who's threatening to nationalize the banking system? Now that's sovereign risk.

If the global fixed-income market appeals to you, you've got two options: U.S. dollar–denominated or local currency (nondollar)–denominated bonds.

Yankee Bonds

Not only have overseas bond markets grown exponentially, but a record number of foreign companies are issuing dollar-denominated debt in the United States. These offerings, known as *Yankee* bonds, are not associated with the baseball team (I couldn't resist). Yankee issuers are not incorporated in the United States and tend to be quasi-government monopolies or companies that have been privatized. That's why international banks dominate this sector, along with industrial giants such as oil companies. As a result, most Yankee bonds receive investment-grade ratings.

Even though Yankee issuers are domiciled abroad, they're required to register with the SEC in order to issue in the United States. For that reason, Yankee issuers are subject to the same regulations as U.S. corporations. That should be comforting to any investor, since SEC financial disclosure rules are typically more rigorous than issuers would encounter in their home countries.

Supranational bonds are also U.S. dollar–denominated international securities, but they're not Yankees. These bonds are from issuers formed to promote economic development and are backed by the federal governments of at least two countries. Consequently, supranational bonds, such as those from the Inter-American Development Bank and the World Bank, are Triple-A rated.

Nondollar Securities

The nondollar bond market has changed significantly over the past 10 years as securities issued in other currencies have become more widely available to individual investors. Truth be told, most investors participate in the nondollar market through mutual funds (we'll discuss them in Chapter 25). The growth of this market, however, provides sophisticated investors with many ways to garner international exposure.

The largest nondollar bond markets are yen (¥, Japan), euro (€, Europe), and sterling (£, Great Britain). Although euro-denominated bonds were first issued in 1999, the euro market has become one of the fastest-growing securities markets in the world. And as it has grown, more U.S. companies have issued euro-denominated bonds. In fact, the twin pillars of the U.S. agency and mortgage securities market— Freddie Mac and Fannie Mae—have both begun to issue agency bonds in euros.

Major corporations, both U.S.- and non–U.S.-based, have recently begun to issue bonds *simultaneously* in different currencies. These are often called *global bonds*, and they have been well received due to the established reputations of their issuers. The large size of these deals also has enhanced liquidity. Global issues are typically denominated in the U.S. dollar, UK sterling, and euro currencies.

Emerging Market Bonds

Sovereign risk is especially pronounced among *emerging market* bonds. This market largely developed subsequent to former U.S. Treasury Secretary Brady's leading role in a plan that initially helped to resolve the Latin American debt crisis in the 1980s. The success of that program, and the *Brady bonds* that were subsequently issued, provided one of the cornerstones for this market sector.

Today, companies and governments from evolving market-based economies issue emerging market securities. These issuers typically are located throughout Latin America, Eastern Europe, and Southeast Asia. These countries are vulnerable to heightened political risk that could threaten the viability of their capital markets. Therefore, the sector is dominated by high-yield securities. The three dominant issuers of emerging market debt currently include Mexico, Brazil, and Russia.

U.S. investors can purchase most sovereign, or government-issued, emerging market debt. Emerging market corporate bonds, though, are another story. That's because most of these securities are treated like high-yield private placements—only qualified institutional buyers need apply. Investors living outside the United States, however, are not subject to these regulations. Occasionally, certain offerings allow U.S. individuals to participate, but you'd be well-advised to steer clear of these bonds unless you're a speculative investor.

Currency Risk

The availability of global securities does not diminish the *currency risk* that's inherent to these investments. In other words, other currencies have the potential to appreciate or depreciate in value when converted back to your home currency. This probably seems familiar if you've traveled overseas (see Figure 20.1).

For example, let's say you purchased 50 euro-denominated (€) corporate bonds with a 6 percent coupon at par. If the dollar and euro were trading at parity (one dollar = one euro), these bonds would cost $50,000. The annual interest payment would be €300, or $300.

$$50 \text{ bonds} \times €1{,}000 \text{ par } = €50{,}000$$

$$€50{,}000 \times 6\% \text{ coupon } = €300 \text{ annual interest}$$

Twelve months later you receive the first €300 payment. However, the euro has since appreciated against the dollar—one euro is now worth 1.05 dollars. What happens when euro interest is converted into US dollars? That's right, you'll get more than $300:

$$€1.00 = \$1.05$$

$$€300 = \$315$$

If instead the dollar had appreciated against the euro, the proceeds would have been less. For example, say one euro was the equivalent of 0.95 dollars. Then:

$$€1.00 = \$0.95$$

$$€300 = \$285$$

FIGURE 20.1   Currency Risk

There are many ways to offset currency risk and to profit from currency fluctuations. But unless you're ready to hire a professional money manager who understands the mechanics of hedging nondollar portfolios, you're not going to be able to do it effectively on your own. Consequently, the best way for most investors to execute a currency strategy is through a mutual fund. For example, U.S. investors could benefit from bond funds invested in euro-denominated securities if the dollar weakened.

Dollar-denominated foreign debt provides US investors with international exposure without incurring direct currency risk. However, since foreign-based issuers operate in their local currencies, keep in mind that you're still indirectly vulnerable to the consequences of a deteriorating exchange rate.

PART FIVE
Peripheral Players

chapter twenty-one
PREFERRED SECURITIES

The Bare Essentials

* *Preferred securities* may be issued as equity or debt.
* A *preferred* has a $25 par value compared to the $1,000 face value of a bond. That's one of the reasons they're so popular with individual investors.
* Preferreds usually feature quarterly payments, rather than the semiannual income streams provided by bonds.

Preferred securities, or *preferreds*, have characteristics that uniquely straddle the debt and equity markets. Until 1993, preferreds were only issued as nonvoting shares of stock, but today they're more frequently issued as debt.

Corporations that issue bonds also commonly issue preferreds. However, preferreds have several notable differences from bonds. The most prominent are their $25 par value, in contrast to the $1,000 par value of bonds. It's one of the reasons they're popular with individual investors—like a low-priced common stock, the $25 price tag just makes them more affordable. Additionally, these securities typically feature a fixed quarterly, rather than semiannual, income stream. Best of all, most preferreds are listed on the New York Stock Exchange, so it's easy to track your holdings. Take that, OTC bond prices!

Preferreds are issued with at least 30 years to maturity and usually have 5 years of call protection. Due to their lengthy maturities, fluctuations in long-term interest rates tend to disproportionately affect prices. Lastly, preferred securities *trade flat*, just like common stock. For that reason, there's no accrued interest.

Credit ratings are assigned to preferreds by the same agencies that rate corporate debt (see Tables 18.2 and 18.3). As a result, an upgrade or a downgrade can significantly affect market value. Given fairly stable market conditions and no change to an issuer's credit rating, preferreds tend to trade within 10 percent to 20 percent of par value. However, a ratings downgrade or a sudden shift in long-term interest rates could easily cause them to trade outside this range.

Equity Preferreds

An equity preferred, or *preferred stock*, is perpetual. That means it never matures, just like common stock, and declares dividends instead of paying interest. Preferred stock is senior to common stock—but subordinate to bonds—in the capital structure (see Table 18.1). Therefore, preferred dividends must be paid before common stock dividends, though not before bondholders receive interest. Since it's an equity security, dividend payments can be suspended at any time, but not before those of common stock. Income generated by some dividend-paying preferreds now qualify for the lowered 15 percent tax rate approved by Congress in May 2003.

Although U.S.-based companies issue most preferreds, more non–U.S. corporations (particularly banks) are issuing them as dollar-denominated securities than ever before. These *Yankee preferreds* usually provide slightly higher yields than comparable domestic issues due to their lack of name recognition and non–U.S. status. Some Yankees are subject to withholding tax. You may be able to get a tax credit for anything that's withheld, but it may be an unpleasant surprise if you expect to receive the full dividend right away.

Another type of perpetual preferred is the *real estate investment trust* (REIT) *preferred*, issued by companies that manage property or real estate loans. There are also *dividend received deduction* (DRD) *preferreds,* so-named because 70 percent of the dividend is offered as a tax break to certain corporate investors that hold them for at least 46 days. Consequently, DRDs typically trade at lower relative yields.

Debt Preferreds

Although preferred stock pays dividends like common stock, *debt preferreds* pay interest like bonds. In fact, many of these preferreds are senior unsecured debt that's structured to resemble a preferred stock. Most debt preferreds are issued at $25 par value and pay quarterly. Since these securities are actually corporate debt, they're senior to traditional equity preferreds. Why do I bore you with such details? Because debt preferreds' standing in the capital structure prevents a company from suspending payments. After all, these are debt securities and, as you know, interest cannot be deferred except in default.

Broker-dealers also create debt preferreds from their own inventory by splitting large blocks of $1,000 par bonds into $25 pieces. Now you know why these preferreds are sometimes called *baby bonds*. Ain't that cute? These repackaged securities pay semiannual interest and may offer incrementally more yield than other preferreds. However, there's a trade-off—these structured issues are comparatively less liquid due to smaller offering sizes and a less active secondary market.

A more common structure is the *trust preferred*. Deeply subordinated debt is placed into a trust, which then issues $25 par securities (some trade in the corporate market at $1,000 face value). Quarterly interest generated by trust preferreds is paid from debt securities held in the trust. Why the funky structure? I'll spare you all the fascinating details, but suffice to say that companies receive substantial tax savings since the interest is tax-deductible.

Although trust preferreds often provide compelling yields, they are junior to the senior debt preferreds just described. Additionally, quarterly payments may be deferred for up to 20 quarters—that's five years to you and me. This deferral period is sometimes called a "dividend holiday"— as if there's anything enjoyable about not receiving money that's been promised to you. Fortunately these holidays rarely occur except in situations of severe financial distress.

Dividends are characterized as *cumulative* or *noncumulative*. Cumulative means that if dividends were suspended and then resumed, missed payments would be repaid; noncumulative means that issuers are allowed to resume regular payments without compensating for lost dividends. However, an issuer would have to first (or simultaneously) suspend dividend payments on its common stock and equity preferreds. This is pretty unlikely since any company that defers interest payments on its preferreds handicaps its ability to access the capital markets.

Other Structures

Adjustable-rate preferreds are perpetual securities, but with a twist; they have a floating, rather than fixed, quarterly dividend. The dividend rate floats between an upper and lower range, or *collar*. If interest rates rise, the dividend rate is adjusted upward. Conversely, the coupon would be adjusted downward if rates declined. There are also *sinking fund preferreds*, which are similar to the bonds we discussed with those redemption provisions. Lastly, there are *convertible preferreds*, but we'll talk about that structure in the next chapter.

Preferred Yields

One of the most common mistakes made by preferred investors is related to yield. Remember our discussion about how current yield misrepresents potential return? Well, it couldn't be more true than in this market—especially when preferreds are trading at a premium. That premium preferred may have a higher coupon but with only five years of call protection, it's likely trading to its short-term call date rather than to its long-term maturity. In other words, there's a chance that the security would be subject to early redemption. So make sure to assess its yield-to-call, *not* its current yield. The easiest way to avoid this mistake? Always ask for yield-to-worst, which will provide you with the lowest possible yield you could expect to receive. That way you're covered.

chapter twenty-two
CONVERTIBLE SECURITIES

The Bare Essentials

- *Convertible securities* are hybrid equity and debt instruments that can be converted from a corporate bond or a preferred security into common stock.
- Although *convertibles* provide semiannual income, their yield is lower than other fixed-income securities in exchange for capital appreciation potential.
- Strict guidelines dictate convertibility.

Say your objective is growth and income—you purchase some stock for $50 a share and some bonds for the semiannual interest. But what if you could accomplish both with one investment? That is, buy a bond that provides semiannual income *and* the option to capture capital gains from a rising stock price? *Convertible bonds*—also known as *convertibles*, or simply *converts*—do just that.

On the surface, convertibles look just like corporate bonds. They are issued by corporations, have final maturity dates, call features, fixed coupons, and semiannual payments. *Convertible preferreds* also are issued. They have similar features to convertible bonds, except income is generated quarterly instead of semiannually. Although convertible securities are structured in different ways, for the most part they are ranked just above preferred stock in the corporate capital structure.

Converts offer more price appreciation potential than traditional debt instruments since investors can swap sleepy bond interest for capital gains. Sounds too good to be true? You're right. In exchange for this benefit, convertible yields are lower than comparable nonconvertible bonds. Additionally, convertibles are issued with a fixed *conversion price*. That's the price at which you'll be able to convert your bonds into common stock. However, since the conversion price is set much higher than the stock price at the time of the offering (you thought they were going to give it away?), the convertible option is worthless if the stock doesn't rise above the conversion price.

If you'd rather walk on the sunny side of the street, think of it this way: convertible securities are bonds with long-term stock options. In other words, you retain the right to redeem the bond at its conversion price until maturity. As opposed to stock options, which are typically short-term, convertibles allow ample time to decide when the rewards of owning the stock outweigh the benefits of holding on to the bond.

The number of shares you can exchange for each convertible bond is dictated by—you guessed it—the conversion price. To figure this out, just divide the bond's par value by its conversion price and you'll produce its *conversion ratio*. For example, if the conversion price were $50, you'll get the following:

$$\frac{\text{Bond's par value}}{\text{Conversion price}} = \text{number of shares}$$

$$\frac{\$1,000}{\$50} = 20 \text{ shares}$$

Since you'd receive 20 shares of common stock for each bond you convert, the conversion ratio is 20:1 (if a stock split occurred, the ratio would adjust accordingly).

Let's elaborate on this a bit further. Say you bought that convertible at par when the common stock was trading at $40. In six months, the stock is still trading at $40, so the option is worthless. The stock finally starts to rise, but then settles exactly at the conversion price of $50. That's called *conversion parity*—the point where the market price of the convertible and the common stock are equal. But there is a happy ending: within the year the stock is trading at $60. So you redeem each of the bonds for 20 shares of common stock and eventually sell your shares at $65. You've managed to lock in a $15 capital gain per share— may we all be so fortunate. Either way, convertible investors benefit if the stock rises and are cushioned from equity routs by its fixed-income features.

However, there is credit risk—they are, after all, corporate bonds. Additionally, convertibles are usually ranked below all other debentures. Lastly, you could also end up with a *busted convert*. As in "broken." That happens when the stock price trades well below the conversion price (it's called being *out-of-the-money*). When that occurs, the convertible option is worthless and the security's price only reflects the intrinsic value of the bond (see Figure 22.1).

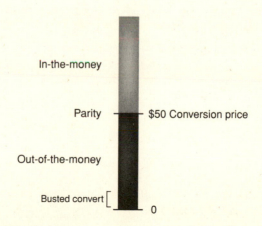

FIGURE 22.1 Convertible Bond

If your objective is growth, you first should consider a company's common stock. However, if that's not appropriate for your portfolio and you're willing to settle for a yield that's lower than its conventional counterpart, a convertible could provide you with the best of both worlds. After all, even if—as Hemingway might say—the stock never rises, it's comforting to know that you could just hold onto the convert, earn semiannual interest, and be repaid principal at maturity.

chapter twenty-three

U.S. SAVINGS BONDS

The Bare Essentials

- *Savings bonds* are issued by the U.S. Treasury Department. There are three types: Series EE, Series I (an inflation-indexed bond), and Series HH/H.
- Although U.S. savings bonds provide the same degree of safety as Treasuries, an active secondary market does not exist.
- U.S. savings bonds are exempt from state and local taxes, and investors may defer paying federal income tax on interest for 30 years or until the bonds are redeemed.

Many of you are probably familiar with U.S. *savings bonds*. They're readily available at local banks and are commonly given as birthday and graduation gifts. But even though these investments are called bonds, they're really not considered part of the bond market. Come again? You read it correctly. Although savings bonds are issued with the same full faith and credit government guarantee enjoyed by Treasuries and retain similar features to other fixed-income securities, they're not bought and sold like other bonds.

In fact, savings bonds are considered *nonmarketable securities* since they're not traded at all in the secondary market. That's why they weren't included in the earlier chapter with other U.S. government issues. *Non-marketable* means that savings bonds may only be bought from, or sold to, the U.S. Treasury or one of its designated agents, such as a local bank or Federal Reserve branch.

Another key difference between savings bonds and the rest of the fixed-income market is that they're registered securities and issue certificates. If you recall, the reason that bonds have a coupon is because, once upon a time, they were registered too. These certificates don't have coupons to clip, but your name and social security number are printed on a certificate and mailed to you. If you purchase a savings bond as a gift for someone else, their name appears on the certificate instead.

Savings bond interest is exempt from state and local taxes. In fact, the U.S. government allows you to defer paying federal taxes on interest for up to 30 years, or until it's redeemed. If you sell a bond before maturity, you are paid accrued interest.

There are three types of savings bonds: Series EE, Series HH/H, and Series I. The letters EE and HH/H, by the way, denote nothing other than the order in which they were created. Conveniently, "I" stands for inflation.

Series EE and Series I

Let's start with Series I, an inflation-indexed savings bond. Its value is pegged to the Consumer Price Index for Urban Consumers (CPI-U). Sound familiar? That's because it's linked to the same inflation indicator as Treasury Inflation Protected Securities (TIPS). Like TIPS, I bonds are a good way to hedge against rising inflation. The I bond yield is actually divided into two parts—a fixed interest rate and an inflation-indexed component that's adjusted every May 1 and November 1.

On the other hand, Series EE bond interest is pegged to Treasuries—it's 90 percent of the six-month average yield on five-year Treasury notes (who knew?). New interest rates for this bond are also announced every May 1 and November 1. However, EE bonds are sold at 50 percent of face value while I bonds are sold at face value. In other words, it would cost $10,000 to purchase a $20,000 Series EE bond. If you wanted to buy a $20,000 Series I bond—well, you get it—it's going to cost you $20,000, and you'll accrue interest on that principal until maturity.

Despite these differences, EE and I bonds have similarities. Each is offered in $50, $75, $100, $200, $500, $1,000, $5,000, and $10,000 denominations. Additionally, both pay variable monthly interest that accrues to principal. This boosts the value of the bond every month, though interest is only compounded semiannually. (Behold!)

A Series I bond earns interest until the end of its 30-year term. EE bonds have a final maturity of 30 years as well, but it's a little different. You see, EE bonds are guaranteed to double and reach their face value within 17 years—designated by the Treasury Department as *original maturity*. If the bond hasn't reached full face value by the end of that term, your bond will be adjusted to compensate for the difference. Then you can either redeem it or continue to earn interest until its final maturity 13 years later.

When your EE bond matures, the difference between the cost and the redemption value must be reported to the IRS so Uncle Sam receives his share. But get this—the U.S. government allows you to defer paying taxes on the EE bond if you exchange those long-awaited proceeds for a 20-year Series HH/H bond. Talk about a long-term savings plan!

The Treasury Department introduced *Patriot Bonds* in 2001 to tap into our national pride. The funny thing about this new bond is that it's not new at all—it's just the same ol' Series EE gussied up in a barely different format. In fact, the *only* difference between EE and this newly created savings bond is the name PATRIOT BOND printed in capital letters between the social security number of the owner and the issuance date. Go ahead and look for yourself (Figure 23.1). You can still see the Series EE markings posted in the top right-hand corner of the savings certificate.

FIGURE 23.1 Patriot Bond

Series HH/H

Series HH/H issues are structured just like traditional interest-paying bonds. You receive par value at maturity and a fixed interest payment (set on the date of purchase) that's paid every six months. That's the main difference between HH/H and the two types already described—since interest is paid to you, its principal does not increase each month. HH/H bonds are offered in $500, $1,000, $5,000, and $10,000 denominations.

And how about this little quirk? You cannot use cash to purchase HH/H bonds. I'm not kidding. The only way to buy these securities is to exchange at least $500 worth of EE bonds, or by using the reinvested proceeds from a Series HH/H that has matured. Go figure. Soon it won't matter anyway since this series is scheduled to be discontinued in 2004.

I'm sure there is one more burning question in your mind; what's with the extra H? I mean, did they have to say it three times? Like having to say New York twice? Here's why: HH bonds have 20-year maturities, while H bonds have 30-year terms.

Purchase and Redemption

All savings bonds offer numerous advantages to investors with long-term savings objectives. Additionally, if a savings bond is used for college tuition in the same year that it is redeemed or matures, accrued interest is exempt from federal taxes (with a few exceptions). The low minimum investment and wide choice of denominations also make these popular gifts. And who could forget their zero default risk?

Series EE and I bonds may be purchased from a bank or the Federal Reserve. You also may purchase them online at Savings Bond Direct (www.savingsbonds.gov). There's no fee and, believe it or not, you can even use a major credit card. Only Series I bonds are currently available on Treasury Direct (www.publicdebt.treas.gov), but credit cards are not accepted. Instead, you'll be required to open a savings bond account (even if you already have one for Treasury purchases). Transactions are debited directly from, or credited to, your bank balance.

Speaking of Treasury Direct, savings bonds purchased there are sold in electronic form only. In fact, the Bureau of Public Debt is currently updating its systems to mirror the book-entry process used by marketable securities. In other words, sometime in the near future, physical certificates no longer will be available. This was prompted by a congressional study that concluded the issuance of these certificates was grossly inefficient and expensive (I imagine the study wasn't cheap, either). Fear not, Series EE and I bond certificates are still available, but the book-entry I bonds offered on Treasury Direct signal the beginning of the end to this age-old practice.

Undoubtedly, one of the great benefits provided by savings bonds is their affordability—you can buy them with as little as $25 (Series EE) or $50 (Series I). Although you are limited to $30,000 face value per calendar year (that means only $15,000 for Series EE), this limit only applies to the registered owner of the bond. For example, you could purchase the maximum $30,000 face amount for, say, three different grandchildren.

Be aware that the minimum holding period was recently increased from six months to one year. Additionally, if you redeem EE or I bonds within the first five years of purchase, you'll lose the last three months of interest as an early withdrawal penalty.

Table 23.1 excludes HH/H bonds since they cannot be purchased outright and they'll soon be obsolete. If you crave more information, call the friendly folks at the U.S. Savings Bond Office (304-480-6112).

TABLE 23.1 Comparison of Series EE and Series I U.S. Savings Bonds

	Series EE	*Series I*
Issued at	50% discount	Full face value
Minimum investment	$25	$50
Denominations	$50, $75, $100, $200, $500, $1,000, $5,000, and $10,000	
Annual purchase limit	$15,000 issue price ($30,000 face value)	$30,000 issue price
Interest rate	90% of 6-month average of 5-year Treasury yield	A fixed rate of return plus a semiannual inflation component
Interest earned	Guaranteed to reach face value in 17 years; earns semiannual interest to 30-year maturity. Interest is paid when bond is redeemed.	Earns semiannual interest to 30-year maturity. Interest is paid when bond is redeemed.
Interest rate adjusted	Rates announced every May 1 and November 1	
Redemption	• Minimum holding period of 1 year • Withdrawal penalty of 3-month interest on bonds redeemed within 5 years	
Tax	Interest exempt from state and local income tax. Federal income tax can be deferred until bonds are redeemed or 30 years, whichever comes first. Federal tax exemption for qualified education expenses.	

chapter twenty-four

CERTIFICATES OF DEPOSIT

The Bare Essentials

- *Certificates of deposit* (CDs) are time deposits created by banks.
- Although CDs have similar characteristics to bonds, CDs are not fixed-income securities since they are not SEC-registered public debt offerings.
- CDs are insured up to $100,000 (interest and principal combined) by the Federal Deposit Insurance Corporation.
- Although banks originate CDs, investors may also purchase them from broker-dealers.

When was the last time you went to the teller window? There's no doubt we're all visiting our local bank branches less frequently—what with those ubiquitous ATM machines and the accessibility of online banking. But if you do happen to drop by, you're likely to be assaulted by signs advertising *certificates of deposit* (CDs). Even though many banks offer other alternatives to traditional savings or money market accounts, CDs remain one of the most important ways they recruit deposits.

Certificates of deposit are heavily marketed at banks since that's where they're created. Technically, these are *time deposits*, not fixed-income securities, because CDs are not SEC-registered offerings. However, bonds and CDs have similar qualities. Most CDs are offered in multiples of $1,000, although *jumbo* CDs are sold in multiples of $100,000. Each has a fixed coupon and a wide range of final maturities. CDs also are available in bullet, callable, and step-up structures.

Insurance

Certificates of deposit are especially popular with individual investors since they are insured by the Federal Deposit Insurance Corporation (FDIC) for up to $100,000 (principal and interest combined). As a result, you'll bear no principal risk. It's just like an insured municipal bond.

Of course, to enjoy the safety of FDIC insurance you can't exceed the $100,000 limit. Investors with more than $100,000 to invest skirt this rule by purchasing multiple CDs at different banking institutions. If that applies to you, remember that the $100,000 represents both principal *and* interest. So you'll have to purchase less than that face amount—say, $95,000—to stay within these bounds.

Maturities

Short-term CDs are commonly sold with three-, six-, nine-month, and one-year maturities. CDs issued under one year pay interest at maturity. CDs also offer 18-month and 2-, 3-, 4-, 5-, 7-, and 10-year maturities. Although 10-year CDs might be tempting due to higher yields, you're typically provided with only one year of call protection. Occasionally, you'll find a 7- to 10-year bullet, but that's the exception, not the rule.

Bank or Broker?

Although CDs are issued and sold by banks, they are commonly distributed by broker-dealers. However, there are two important differences between purchasing a CD at a bank or at a brokerage firm. First, CDs bought directly from a bank usually trigger a penalty—typically 6 or 12 months of interest—if you redeem before maturity. When you purchase a CD from a broker, an early withdrawal penalty is not charged.

That being said, if you attempt to sell a CD to a broker-dealer before it matures, you'll be offered its current value in the secondary market; just like when you sell a bond. In fact, your CD could be trading below your cost basis. Under special circumstances, such as death or mental disability, CDs may be "put" back, or redeemed, at par value. This is similar to the corporate MTN survivor's option we discussed earlier, except CDs do not have holding periods for this benefit.

Another important distinction between buying a CD from a bank or broker is the way interest is paid. Banks pay compound interest that is received at redemption, while brokers pay simple interest every six months. For example, a five-year CD with a 6 percent coupon would yield $350 compounded *daily* interest, compared to $300 simple interest. Consequently, if generating extra income is not your objective, and you plan to hold the CD until maturity, you'll usually earn more interest compounding the investment at a bank. However, if your goal is to supplement current income, then you should consider purchasing a CD from a broker.

chapter twenty-five

FUNDS AND UNIT INVESTMENT TRUSTS

The Bare Essentials

🍀 Three types of bond funds are available: *mutual funds, closed-end funds,* and *unit investment trusts* (*UIT*s).

🍀 Mutual funds and closed-end funds are actively managed bond portfolios, while UITs comprise a fixed group of bonds held in a trust.

🍀 Mutual funds and closed-end funds are perpetual, while UITs mature. Each provides a monthly income stream.

🍀 Although no fund should be chosen by cost alone, it behooves investors to thoroughly review expenses prior to any investment.

No investment book would be complete without a discussion about funds. According to the Investment Company Institute, nearly $1.5 trillion is invested in over 2,000 taxable and tax-exempt bond funds. And that's excluding money market funds (which we'll discuss in the next chapter). This universe is so deep and diverse that you could easily dedicate an entire book to the subject (others have). I'll try to cover the essentials in one chapter.

Three types of bond funds are available: *mutual funds, closed-end funds,* and *unit investment trusts,* (UITs). You are probably familiar with mutual funds: they're the most popular type, constituting the majority of available investment options in self-directed retirement plans, such as a 401(k) or 403(b). *Exchange-traded funds* (ETFs), which usually mirror indexes such as the S&P 500, also are available. However, since nearly all ETFs are stock funds, we'd hardly be taking the bare essential approach by discussing them here.

There are a number of differences among the three types of funds. In the broadest sense, mutual and closed-end funds are actively managed bond portfolios. A UIT, in contrast, comprises a fixed group of bonds held in a trust that is not actively managed. All three are designed to attract investors with objectives that match the fund's strategy. For example, a municipal bond fund attracts investors looking for tax-free income, while a high-yield fund attracts speculative investors seeking high taxable income and capital gains. Bond funds invest in nearly every type of fixed-income security available, except for CDs.

When you purchase a fund, you'll automatically be sent a prospectus. (As we discussed earlier, the prospectus is a valuable tool that familiarizes you with specific investment guidelines and objectives.) Better yet, you can request the prospectus prior to your purchase. That way, you'll be fully informed *before* you invest.

Net Asset Value

Mutual funds are bought and sold at *net asset value* (NAV). The fund company determines NAV by subtracting expenses from the fund's total value, and then dividing by the number of outstanding shares. The current NAV is determined at the end of each business day—it's conveniently listed on the fund's website and in major daily newspapers. Mutual funds are known as open-end funds since they issue an unlimited number of shares. Although these funds are distributed through investment firms, shares are actually bought and sold by the fund company itself. For that reason, NAV is dictated by both the performance of the underlying securities and, to a lesser degree, by investor demand. For instance, widespread redemptions could contribute to lower NAV since holdings in the fund would have to be sold. By law, mutual fund companies are required to provide daily liquidity to their shareholders.

Closed-end funds, on the other hand, are transacted like stocks. That means shares are not bought and sold directly by the fund company. Instead, the number of shares traded is fixed at its initial offering and usually trades with a bid/ask spread on a stock exchange, such as the NYSE. For that reason, closed-end fund prices reflect investor demand and market sentiment rather than the underlying value of the fund's fixed-income securities. Just like bonds rarely trade at par, these funds typically trade above or (mostly) below NAV. Be aware that many closed-end funds are *leveraged*. That means they raise additional capital by issuing securities, such as preferred stock, since a closed-end fund cannot issue more shares. Although this generates a higher yield for investors, using leverage is just like having a margin account—it could be beneficial when the market is rising, but it could just as easily exacerbate losses if the fund were faced with difficult market conditions.

Unit investment trusts are issued with a fixed number of shares. Since there is no active secondary market for UITs, you'll have to sell shares directly to the issuer if you want to redeem them prior to maturity. The bid would reflect current net asset value as determined by the issuer.

Active versus Passive Management

Mutual funds and closed-end funds are actively managed by investment professionals known as *portfolio managers*. Although portfolio managers have discretion to purchase or sell securities, they must adhere to a specific set of investment guidelines. For example, an investment-grade corporate bond fund might prohibit the purchase or retention of any securities rated below Triple-B. Consequently, if a Triple-B bond were downgraded to Double-B, the portfolio manager would be compelled to sell it.

A UIT is much less diversified than a mutual or closed-end fund—it could comprise as few as 10 different issues. Bonds bought for the trust are selected and monitored by investment professionals, but the portfolio's initial composition does not change. If a special circumstance occurs—such as when an issuer appears headed for default—the bond would be sold, but not replaced with another security. Instead, the principal would be distributed to shareholders. Due to the fixed composition of the portfolio, it's especially important to judge a UIT by the *quality* of its underlying securities, *not* by its yield.

Perpetual versus Fixed Maturity

Mutual fund and closed-end fund shares are perpetual, just like common stocks. That means they don't have a maturity date—which, of course, contradicts one of the most compelling reasons to purchase individual bonds.

Unit investment trusts are different. They have predictable lifespans, usually from 10 to 30 years, since the bonds in the trust are fixed and have defined maturities. Sometimes UITs are marketed with a final maturity, but don't get confused—that merely represents the maturity of the longest bond in the portfolio. If callable bonds are included in the trust, declining interest rates could cause early redemptions and a lower overall yield. Toward the end of its term, principal is gradually returned to the investor as each bond in the UIT matures.

Income

Funds contain a variety of bond issues that together generate interest throughout the year. That's why fund investors receive monthly income streams, although active portfolio management inevitably causes payments to fluctuate. Since there are many ways to determine yield, funds are required to calculate and disclose a standard *SEC yield*. This ensures that investors are able to fairly assess potential return by comparing yields of different funds on an apples-to-apples basis. Whether NAV rises or declines, investors also receive capital gains distributions. This generally occurs at year-end due to the sale of securities in the fund that increased in value.

The majority of UITs provide monthly payments. The interest income remains fairly constant since the composition of its portfolio is fixed. That is, until any bonds are called or mature.

Expenses

Butterflies might be free, but bond funds are not. Let's start with UITs, since they are pretty straightforward. UITs do not charge annual management fees—after all, there is no manager. Although maintenance fees are typically low (usually less than 50 basis points), upfront sales charges on these funds are not—they usually range from 3 to 5 percent.

Now let's move onto mutual funds, which have much more complex fee structures. First of all, many funds have an upfront or back-end sales charge known as a *load* (those that don't are *no-load* funds). Loads typically range between 2 percent and 5 percent of your total investment, which is debited automatically when you purchase or sell a fund. For example, if you invested $100,000 in a fund with a 3 percent upfront load, the cost would be $3,000. As a result, your initial investment is actually $97,000.

That's the easy part. Problem is, mutual funds often have several different share classes—typically A, B, and C—each with a different schedule of charges. Additionally, many mutual funds charge graduated loads depending on the amount or time invested. For instance, you might pay as little as 2 percent if you invest at least $250,000, but as much as 5 percent if you invest less than $100,000. Back-end loads, also known as deferred sales charges, usually depend on the time invested. Fo instance, there might not be an exit fee if you remained invested for at least five years. But the same fund might charge, say, 2 percent if you redeem after three years and 4 percent for shares held less than one year.

Many funds also charge *12b1 fees*, which pay for promotional and general marketing expenses. These fees do not exceed 25 basis points for no-load funds, and are limited to 100 basis points for load funds. Funds with front-end and back-end loads average 50 and 100 basis points of 12b1 fees, respectively. The annual expense fee that's automatically charged to cover the fund's overhead is included in the *expense ratio*, which is simply total expenses divided by the assets in the fund. All else being equal, investors should target low expense ratios. For instance, if annual expenses totaled $7 million and the size of the fund was $700 million, the expense ratio would be 1 percent. If expenses were instead $14 million, the expense ratio would be 2 percent.

Closed-end funds come in many varieties and are subject to different fees and expenses. You will always pay a commission, though, since they all trade on a stock exchange.

Although funds should not be selected on costs alone, some are more onerous than others. After all, embedded charges erode your total return, so be sure to take a hard look at them. Be wary of high fees or expense ratios since they are not modified even when funds perform poorly. For a quick and easy way to estimate and compare the complex world of fund expenses, use the *SEC Mutual Fund Cost Calculator* (www.sec.gov).

A Final Note on Funds

This chapter was especially tough to write since there's simply so much to say about fund investing. But that's outside the scope of this book (perhaps a *Naked Guide to Mutual Funds?*). When I want more information about bond funds, I simply go to www.pimco.com. Pacific Investment Management Company (PIMCO) is not only the largest mutual fund company specializing in bonds, but it also has a user-friendly website chock full of information about the bond market.

TABLE 25.1   Fund Comparisons

	Mutual	*Closed-End*	*UIT*
Portfolio management	Active	Active	Passive
Price	Daily NAV	Shares trade on stock exchange	Bid/offer from issuer
Maturity	Perpetual	Perpetual	Matures
Number of shares	Unlimited	Fixed	Fixed
Income	Monthly	Monthly	Monthly
Purchase/ redemption	Mutual fund company	Stock exchange	Issuer
Distribution	Mutual fund company/ brokerage firm	Brokerage firm	Issuer/ brokerage firm
Fees	Management fee and load/no-load	Management fee and commission	No management fee load

Try to keep in mind that you should be no less diligent about fund investing than you if you purchased a bond, especially regarding expenses. Forgive me for repeating myself, but to make the right decision I implore you—*read the prospectus first* (see Table 25.1).

A Few Words about Managed Accounts

Some investors who have the financial resources to construct a large bond portfolio opt for managed accounts. These accounts usually require a minimum investment of $100,000 to $250,000. The proceeds are then either turned over to a professional money manager or are allocated among several different portfolio managers to match a strategy that would help achieve the stated investment objectives. An annual fee is charged for the privilege, typically from 75 to 125 basis points of the total account value.

chapter twenty-six

MONEY MARKET FUNDS

The Bare Essentials

* Money market mutual funds provide individuals with access to higher-yielding cash-equivalent instruments.

* These funds provide a higher rate of return than savings accounts, usually offer check-writing privileges, and are readily available as cash.

* Money market funds invest in short-term securities, such as Treasury bills, CDs, *banker's acceptances*, and *commercial paper*.

Until the early 1970s, you basically had three places to park your cash: a checking account, a savings account, or under your mattress. Institutional investors, meanwhile, had access to a wide range of higher-yielding, short-term fixed-income securities.

That's why money market mutual funds were created—to provide access to higher-yielding cash-equivalent instruments. Although money markets are administered like other mutual funds—complete with prospectus, portfolio manager, and shares—there is an important difference: Their share price (NAV) remains constant at $1.00 per share. This is not mandated by law, but "breaking the buck" is contrary to industry practice. Of course, it is possible for NAV to fall below $1.00 if the underlying securities perform poorly. But that's extraordinarily rare. In fact, it only happened once since these types of funds were created. Since money market funds can also provide check-writing privileges, have a higher rate of return than savings accounts, and are readily available as cash, it's no wonder they've become enormously popular.

Money market funds are available at banks, brokerage firms, and directly from mutual fund companies. Banks offer federal insurance on these funds for up to $100,000 (that's right, just like CDs). However, you're better off with the higher yields offered by mutual funds and brokerage firms since these investments pose minimal principal risk anyway. Just like the mutual funds we discussed in the last chapter, money markets are also quoted with a standardized SEC yield. This calculation annualizes the average interest rate offered by the fund for the last seven days.

Money market fund yields are commonly posted in major newspapers. Most financial institutions routinely sell money markets to their customers. That means even if you're not an active investor, chances are you've got cash sitting in a money market account right now. But did you ever stop to think about what the heck a money market fund really is?

Money Market Securities

Money market funds are primarily differentiated by the underlying securities in which they invest. They are subject to strict federal guidelines that limit investments to high-quality securities issued by U.S. corporations, as well as U.S. federal, state, and local governments. Additionally, an SEC rule stipulates that securities in these funds cannot mature beyond 397 days, and the dollar-weighted average maturity of the fund's holdings cannot exceed 90 days.

Treasury bills, floaters, and short-term CDs are all purchased for money market funds. Since we discussed these securities earlier, we won't elaborate on them here. Another money market instrument is a *banker's acceptance* (BA). In all likelihood, you've never heard of a BA unless you are an importer or exporter. These one- to six-month securities are sold at a discount and reflect the creditworthiness of the issuing bank that guarantees payment at maturity.

Then there's *commercial paper* (CP). Individual investors do not directly participate in this market because the minimum trade size runs as high as $25 million. Commercial paper is issued by large public companies for a maximum of 270 days as a cost-effective alternative to short-term bank borrowing. Since CP is corporate debt, the rating agencies rank the credit quality of each issuer. However, just like short-term municipal debt, CP has its own ratings scale (see Table 26.1).

Money market fund portfolio managers are subject to investment guidelines that restrict them to the two highest CP rating categories. Moreover, no more than 5 percent of total assets may be invested in second tier A-2/P-2 securities (S&P ratings are conventionally listed first in the CP market). Since mutual funds are such large buyers of CP, a downgrade to A2/P-2 (or lower) can significantly impact the short-term borrowing plans of major issuers.

Other short-term money market instruments include agency discount notes, which were discussed earlier, and *repurchase agreements*, or *repos*. These are arrangements to sell securities with the agreement to buy them back (usually overnight) at a specific price.

Mutual fund companies and brokerage firms also offer *tax-exempt money market funds*, which invest in short-term Treasury and municipal debt. These fall into two categories: federally tax-exempt funds or

TABLE 26.1   Commercial Paper Rankings

	S&P	*Moody's*	*Risk Characteristics*
Investment-Grade	A-1+/A-1	P-1	Strong quality
	A-2	P-2	Satisfactory quality
	A-3	P-3	Adequate quality
Non-Investment-Grade	B	NP	Not prime / poor quality
	C		Currently vulnerable to default
	R		Under regulatory supervision
	SD/D		Selective default / default

single-state funds that also provide state and local tax exemptions. Of course, yields offered by tax-exempt funds are lower than their taxable counterparts.

Money Market Funds and Inflation

Since the average maturity of a money market fund must be three months or less, its yield is directly tied to prevailing short-term interest rates. Sometimes money market rates even fall below the inflation rate. In that case, you're faced with a negative real interest rate.

For example, let's say inflation is 2.5 percent and money markets yield 1.5 percent. Survey says? That's right, you'd be earning (or more accurately, not earning) a −1.0 percent real rate of interest. In effect, your purchasing power is declining by 1.0 percent each year. Of course, it's better than storing cash under your mattress. But if you've got a significant amount of money failing to keep pace with inflation—and you don't need access to it immediately—it's time to consider some higher-yielding alternatives. This has become an especially timely concern in 2003 since money market yields have recently fallen to historical lows.

PART SIX
Putting It All Together

chapter twenty-seven

HAVE AN INFORMED OPINION

The Bare Essentials

🍂 Uninformed investors are more likely to get blindsided.

🍂 There are many resources available to help investors gain a basic understanding of the financial markets.

🍂 You'll make better investment decisions if you're informed since you won't be captive to someone else's views.

What do you think about the economy? The direction of interest rates? A stock or bond market rally? The next winner of the World Series? You get the idea; have an opinion. Better yet, have an informed opinion.

Alright, that may be stating the obvious, but allow me to digress for a moment. To make investment decisions in a vacuum is like taking a test without studying—you might still pass, but odds are you'll do a heckuva lot better if you are prepared.

For example, let's say you're unaware that interest rates are widely forecast to rise in the coming months. Perhaps you just go ahead and buy some 30-year bonds while informed investors are wisely avoiding long-duration securities. If rates dropped instead, well, you're a hero since you picked up bonds at fire sale prices. Congratulations, but that's called *luck*. However, if you disagreed with consensus and purchased long maturities because you thought rates would decline, that's called being a *contrarian investor*. Big difference. In both cases you're right, but if you're informed, you'll be right more often.

So how can you become an informed investor? Well, it happens in small doses, over time. For example, the next time the Federal Reserve chairman is featured on the news, pay close attention to the commentary. When you read the newspaper tomorrow morning and flip past the business section, go back and review that table of Treasury yields. Have they been rising or declining? Then take a moment to ask yourself *why* before moving on.

You could even read the daily "Credit Markets" column in the *Wall Street Journal* (*WSJ*). Or check out the upcoming municipal and corporate bond offerings in Monday's *WSJ* and *New York Times*. Or, if you're partial to weekly periodicals, purchase *Barron's* over the weekend for complete market coverage.

And let's not forget the Internet. The next time you've finished checking e-mail, swing over to a financial web site, such as *CNBC* (http://moneycentral.msn.com/home.asp) or *Bloomberg* (www.bloomberg.com), and spend a few minutes catching up on market news. Want to find out more about the Federal Reserve (http://www.federalreserve.gov) or the Treasury Department (http://www.ustreas.gov)? More about the latest developments in the bond market? The Bond Market Association is a font of information (www.investinginbonds.com). Interested in knowing what the rating agencies are thinking? See for yourself at www.moodys.com, www.standardandpoors.com, and www.fitchibca.com. Most investment firms and mutual fund companies are also online. Their sites are full of research and education about stocks, bonds, and the economy.

The resources available to you are endless. Whatever your path to knowledge, developing an informed opinion provides a framework that allows you to make better investment decisions. Don't get me wrong—I'm not advocating you ignore financial experts who you've come to respect. To the contrary, a trusted advisor is a great benefit. However, you'll be a more successful investor if you're able to integrate your own views rather than just being captive to someone else's.

chapter twenty-eight

ESTABLISH A FRAMEWORK

The Bare Essentials

🍃 Setting specific goals is the first step to investment success.

🍃 Assess how much risk you're willing to tolerate *before* you invest. Are you conservative, moderate, aggressive, or speculative?

🍃 Structuring a portfolio to match your personal framework is one of the most effective ways to reach your goals.

🍃 Clearly assess your goals and risk profile *before* choosing whether to consult a financial advisor or go it alone.

🍃 Investment decisions should be based on quality, not cost. Remember, the least expensive way is not necessarily the best way.

Determine Your Goals

When you pull out of the driveway, do you have any idea where you're headed? Of course you do. Otherwise you'd be driving around aimlessly. Yet, that's exactly what many investors are inclined to do—invest without any sense of direction. It's not only one of the most common investment mistakes, but it's also one of the most destructive. Think about it: If you don't know where you're headed, how are you ever going to get there? Correction—you'll get there. But wherever it is, it'll be a surprise. And who wants to stake their hard-earned savings on a surprise ending? As Clint Eastwood would say, "Are you feeling lucky?"

Rather than set yourself astray, take a step back and establish some specific goals before rushing headlong into the market. Start with the following question: "What am I trying to accomplish?" To answer this, consider these objectives:

- Growth

- Capital preservation

- Income

Growth is better achieved in the equity market, but the fixed-income market is better equipped for the last two goals. For example, if you're planning for retirement, bonds provide an effective way to safeguard financial assets. If you need to supplement current income, bonds generate predictable payment streams.

Of course, multiple goals rarely fit neatly into the same time frame. That's why it's important to further characterize your objectives as *short-term, intermediate-term* or *long-term*. For example, the down payment required for the house you want to purchase next year would be a short-term goal. A long-term objective could be college tuition savings for your 2-year-old twins. I know—your children are going to get academic or sports scholarships. I'm sure they're very talented, but just in case, you should set some money aside. At the very least, you'll have a more prosperous retirement.

Speaking of children and retirement, your age should also help dictate investment objectives. For instance, if you're retiring in five years, the composition of your portfolio naturally should be geared toward capital preservation. However, if you're only 35 years old, it could be more oriented toward growth.

Try not to underestimate the importance of this basic exercise because each goal potentially dictates a different investment approach. And each approach requires a different strategy. In other words, you must proactively shape the process in order to produce the stated intent.

Assess Your Risk Profile

Let's face it—nobody's entirely comfortable with risk, but some are more tolerant than others. That's why it's important to honestly assess how much risk you're willing to tolerate *before* you invest. To do this, ask yourself: "What kind of investor am I? How do I react when faced with uncertainty? How about volatility?"

Structuring a portfolio to match your emotional framework is one of the most effective ways to reach your goals simply because it fosters peace of mind. What does sleeping well at night have to do with success in the bond market? Think of it this way: If you have peace of mind, you are less likely to react irrationally when markets are volatile, which inevitably results in poor investment decisions. A secure mindset also shelters you from the two qualities that can wreak havoc on any good investment plan: *fear* and *greed*. Of course, avoiding these temptations is easier said than done, and even the most experienced investors occasionally fall victim to the twin sirens.

Investment firms typically characterize client risk profiles as *conservative, moderate, aggressive,* or *speculative.* Of course, you might be conservative with your children's college tuition savings, but aggressive with some extra cash you'd like to invest in junk bonds. That's fine— these are not hard-and-fast categories. But these profiles do help financial advisors guide their clients toward the most appropriate investments. So, whether you're conservative, speculative, or somewhere in between, just remember one thing—if you're comfortable with your investments by day, you'll sleep better at night.

Financial Advisor or Do-It-Yourself?

Once upon a time, investors had few alternatives but to call a broker to participate in the bond market. Mutual funds were not widely available, discount investment services did not exist, and the Internet wasn't even a glimmer in Al Gore's eye. Today you can still call a broker. But you also can deal directly with mutual fund companies, transact throu discount brokers and online services, hire fee-only planners, or work with a bank trust department. Essentially, all these options boil down to one basic choice—enlist the help of a financial advisor, or go it alone.

With the advent of more market coverage—particularly on television and the Internet—the do-it-yourself attitude has multiplied exponentially. Better-educated and more informed investors, combined with a proliferation of discount brokerage firms and the accessibility of online investing, only reinforced this trend. Although the do-it-yourself attitude has somewhat diminished since the end of the bull market in 2000, the sense that we should go it alone still permeates the mindset of many individuals. Perhaps even you.

In an ideal world we'd all be able to select the most appropriate investments on our own. In reality, of course, it's simply not the case. Not because we're unable to do so, but because other priorities—such as busy work and family lives—detract from the attention that's required to properly manage an investment portfolio. Frankly, it amazes me how many ill-equipped and uninformed investors confidently forge ahead without financial advice. Like accidents waiting to happen. Think about it—just because you've watched *Court TV*, would you defend yourself in a court of law? Or because you've logged hours on a medical web site, are you prepared to diagnose and treat yourself when you're ill?

Don't get me wrong—you may have the wherewithal to tackle bond investments on your own. Perhaps you're an experienced stock investor and possess the qualities that foster success: a long-term outlook, the discipline to stay informed, and the capacity to segregate emotions from your investment decisions. However, if you don't possess those qualities, or if you're unsure, you should seriously consider working with a professional.

By the way, many investors allow cost to dictate their investment choices. It's a mistake. That might sound counterintuitive—after all, who wants to spend more than they have to? But remember, *you get what you pay for*. The least expensive way is not necessarily the best way. It could cost less initially, but—mark my words—the wrong route is going to cost you more in the long run than if you'd bought the right fund or paid for the best advice in the first place.

Before you sit down and write me an angry letter, be aware that I'm not suggesting no-load mutual funds or low-fee financial advisors are bad investment choices. What matters is *how* you arrive at that choice. For example, if you require estate planning, working with a bank trust department may make perfect sense. If a friend has had success with a financial advisor, it might be worth the extra cost. If you find a highly ranked mutual fund that meets your objectives *and* it's no-load, well, that's the best of both worlds. You get the idea—to judge what's best, *start with quality, not with cost.*

chapter twenty-nine

DIVERSIFICATION

The Bare Essentials

- There is simply no better way to put it: *Don't put all your eggs in one basket.*
- Diversification suggests that the overall rate of return may be improved—and risk substantially reduced—if a portfolio is populated with a number of uncorrelated investments.
- There are a number of ways to diversify—by security type, industry, issuer, geography, and currency.

You know the old saying, "Don't put all your eggs in one basket"? Well, that about sums up diversification—don't stake your life savings on one investment. Essentially, diversification works because it spreads out the risk that's inherent to investing. It's simply the most important concept to keep in mind as you develop an investment strategy. But don't take my word for it—Harry Markowitz was awarded the 1990 Nobel Prize in Economics for this theory.

Of course, it's much more exciting to find the next hot stock or bond offering, invest your life savings in it, and then wait to make a killing. After all, the more you invest, the more you'll gain. Right? In case you missed it, the operative word in that sentence above is "killing." Diversification requires giving up that potential killing, but it also eliminates a potentially larger loss.

Now don't get me wrong, I'd like to win the lottery too. But even though Powerball is fun to play, the odds of winning are so remote that I'm not going to count on it for my retirement, and neither should you.

How Diversification Works

Diversification suggests that the overall rate of return may be improved; and risk substantially reduced, if a portfolio is populated with a number of uncorrelated investments. Securities that behave differently under similar market conditions are considered uncorrelated. For example, the safety afforded by Treasuries would balance the higher volatility and potential capital losses inherent in stock investing.

Segmenting a portfolio into different types of investments is known as *asset allocation*. In fact, many investment firms provide models that recommend how much of your portfolio should be allocated to each major asset class—usually stocks, bonds, and cash (which includes cash equivalents like money market funds) (see Figure 29.1). Some also recommend a small exposure to commodities, such as gold. Asset allocation recommendations are modified whenever an investment firm announces a significant change to its economic or market outlook.

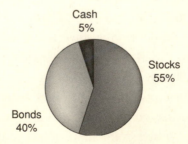

FIGURE 29.1   Asset Allocation Model

Diversifying a Bond Portfolio

The easiest way to diversify a bond portfolio is to purchase different *security types*. For instance, you could buy agencies to offset risk and smooth out unpredictable returns in a high-yield bond portfolio. You could add international bonds to hedge domestic holdings, or corporates and mortgages to supplement a portfolio of Treasury securities. Figure 29.2 shows some sample portfolios tailored by risk profile.

Some investment firms even provide online questionnaires that help you customize a blend of securities that would be right for you. These software programs typically require you to quantify your risk profile, objectives, and time horizon to help determine the right asset allocation.

After you've determined what types of bonds are best for your portfolio, you could further diversify by *industry*. Of course this doesn't apply to Treasuries, but it's important for corporate and municipal bond investors because of credit risk. For example, suppose you're ready to invest $75,000 in corporate bonds. Instead of, say, putting the entire amount in auto manufacturing bonds, you could split the proceeds three ways to include energy and consumer product issuers. This helps to offset event risk. If you have a tax-exempt portfolio, you could choose among education, healthcare, industrial development, transportation and utility bonds. Depending on the size of your portfolio, you could also diversify within each industry by *issuer*.

FIGURE 29.2 Sample Bond Portfolios

Diversifying by issuer also makes sense for municipal bond investors. After all, municipalities have varying degrees of credit quality. Diversification especially applies to revenue bond holdings because of their vulnerability to higher costs or lower usage. Muni buyers should also diversify by *geography* to lessen dependence on any one region. That means purchasing outside your immediate area and considering both out-of-state and U.S. commonwealth issues—such as from Puerto Rico—that provide similar tax benefits.

Speaking of geography, international portfolios could be diversified by *currency*. For instance, you could purchase Fannie Mae bonds or mutual funds that are denominated in euros rather than U.S. dollars. Additionally, you could diversify by *maturity* and *structure* to offset reinvestment and call risk—but we'll talk more about that later when we discuss strategies in Part 7.

Lastly, it might be appropriate to diversify a portfolio of individual bonds with mutual funds. For instance, suppose you want to add mortgage-backed exposure to your agency and investment-grade corporate bond portfolio. However, you're not confident in your ability to choose or manage mortgage securities. That's when a fund makes sense. Mutual funds are especially relevant for volatile bond sectors that require the most diversification, such as high-yield or emerging market bonds. This still allows you to participate without turning your hair gray. That is, unless it's already gray like mine.

No matter how you slice it, diversification gives you an opportunity to minimize the potential loss in any one security by spreading market risk across many different investments. Bottom line? Successful investors gamble in Vegas, not in the bond market.

chapter thirty

INTERPRETING THE YIELD CURVE

The Bare Essentials

- Analyzing the Treasury yield curve helps to identify which maturities provide the best values.
- To determine the best part of curve, think about the following questions: *What are your objectives? What's your interest rate outlook? Are you being paid to extend?*
- Analysis of the curve is most useful when integrated with your own objectives.
- The yield curve also is used to identify value in other bond market sectors.

One of the most common questions I'm asked is: "Where is the best part of the curve?" In other words, what's the best maturity to buy? Problem is, the answer differs depending on your responses to the following questions: What are your objectives? What's your interest rate outlook? Are you being paid to extend? Given our discussion in previous chapters, I'll assume you've already answered the first two questions. So let's g ahead and answer the third.

As we learned earlier, the yield curve's slope is usually positive, with yields increasing as maturities lengthen (see Figure 30.1). Bond analysts commonly track spreads between 2- and 10-year notes, as well as 2-year notes and 30-year bonds. For example, in Figure 30.1, the 2-year yield is 3.5 percent, the 10-year is 5.0 percent, and the 30-year is 6.0 percent. As a result, the 2- to 10-year spread is 150 basis points (bp) and the 2-to-30-year spread is 250 bp. If the 20-year averages for 2- to 10-year and 2- to 30-year spreads are approximately 87 bp and 113 bp, respectively, are you being paid to extend? *Getting paid to extend* refers to the incremental yield you receive by purchasing longer-dated maturities. Since these spreads exceed their historical averages, you're being fairly compensated for purchasing beyond 2 years out on the curve.

It helps to have a historical perspective, but even without data you can usually eyeball where the curve starts flattening to identify *how far* it pays to extend. For instance, notice how wide the spread is between the 2- and 10-year notes. That steepness implies you're being fairly compensated for investing in a longer maturity. Now take a look at the difference between 10- and 30-year yields. Are you being paid to extend? Perhaps, but you're only being compensated by 100 bp to extend another 20 years.

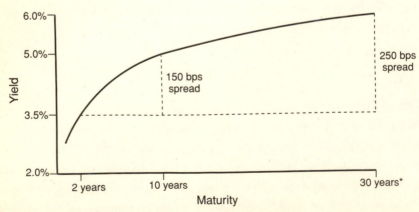

* The last auction of the 30-year Treasury bond was on February 15, 2001.

E 30.1   Yield Curve Spreads

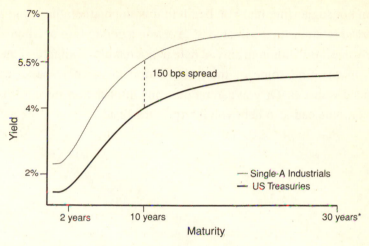

FIGURE 30.2   Treasury and Corporate Bond Yield Curves

Reading the curve is most valuable when you integrate it with your investment objectives. For example, let's say the 5-year note appears to be the most compelling. But what's compelling about it if you have a specific liability that's 15 years away? Don't laugh, it happens all the time. Investors learn about the "best value" on the curve and then just go ahead and buy it. That kind of strategy works for traders who are paid to capture market inefficiencies. But if you're a buy-and-hold investor, it only makes sense if the maturity is consistent with your specific goals and interest rate outlook.

The yield spread between Treasuries and other bond sectors is commonly used by bond analysts to identify value. To determine whether corporate bonds are *rich* (overvalued) or *cheap* (undervalued), we compare their yields with similar Treasury maturities and evaluate the difference.

For example, if the spread between 10-year Single-A industrials and 10-year Treasuries has historically been 100 bp, then a 150 bp spread implies that corporate bonds are cheap (see Figure 30.2). On the other hand, if the spread narrowed to 50 bp, then corporates would be rich

I'm not suggesting that you begin timing the market, but being aware of spread relationships will at least give you a good sense of a bond's relative value. And although spread data is not readily available to the public, you can find some of this information in the newspaper and on financial websites. Or you can request this information from a financial advisor, who can also help you interpret the results.

chapter thirty-one
MANAGING VOLATILITY

The Bare Essentials

* Duration provides an effective way to manage volatility in bond and mutual fund portfolios. However, *it does not account for differences in credit quality.*
* Among the most important rules of thumb are:
  * Duration generally rises as maturity lengthens.
  * Bullets typically have longer durations than comparable callables.

Many events quickly heighten bond market volatility, such as an unexpected announcement from the Federal Reserve or the release of surprisingly strong (or weak) economic data. Unfortunately, there's nothing you can do to control most of these factors—they are just part and parcel of being a fixed-income investor. But remember the saying, "God grant me the power to change the things that I can, and the wisdom to accept the things that I cannot"? Well, there are things you can change to manage price volatility.

As we discussed earlier, duration is the best way to gauge a bond's price sensitivity to interest rates. In general, bonds with shorter maturities have lower durations and are subsequently less sensitive to changes in interest rates. For instance, to lower a portfolio's duration without liquidating longer maturities, purchase securities with shorter durations to offset interest rate risk. Even if the durations of some bonds remain high, increased diversification allows you to smooth out overall volatility. Additionally, some funds feature short-term, medium-term, and long-term duration strategies. You can combine these in your portfolio to be diversified by duration.

You can use duration to evaluate a bond portfolio or mutual fund. In order to do this, a weighted average is derived from the unique duration of each security to estimate overall volatility.

However, duration has one major drawback: *It does not account for differences in credit quality*. All else being equal, higher-quality bonds (such as Triple-A) are less volatile than lower-quality bonds (such as Double-B) with similar durations. Additionally, bonds with good liquidity trade frequently and have tighter spreads; price swings tend to be less exaggerated as the liquidity of a bond improves.

Higher coupons produce more stability among investments of equal maturity and credit quality. Of course, you'll have to pay a hefty premium for the privilege—sometimes well above par. But these bonds will generate more interest and be better equipped to cushion any price depreciation if rates rise. Additionally, more cash flow is available for reinvestment at higher rates.

In summary, here are some guidelines to follow:

- Duration generally rises as maturity lengthens.
- Long-duration bonds tend to be the most volatile, while short-duration bonds provide more price stability.
- Bullet bonds typically have longer durations than comparable callables due to potential early redemption.
- Bonds with lower coupons tend to have higher durations. Consequently, zero coupon securities tend to be the most volatile bond structure.
- Duration is always shorter than a bond's final maturity, except for zero coupons. For zeros, duration is equal to maturity.

- All else being equal, higher-quality bonds exhibit less volatility than lower-quality bonds.

- Bonds with good liquidity generally demonstrate lower volatility.

Put Your Concerns in Perspective

Let's just take a moment to put all this volatility talk into its proper perspective. Since interest rates are bound to rise and fall over time, the value of your bond investment is going to fluctuate. But if you muster the discipline to look away from these inevitable price changes when there's no fundamental deterioration in credit quality, you'll enjoy the distinct advantages that bond investments provide. That is, if you're a buy-and-hold investor and purchase high-quality bonds, you needn't be unduly concerned about normal price swings. Because unlike the uncertainty associated with stocks, your bond interest is still going to be paid like clockwork and your principal returned at maturity.

PART SEVEN
Getting Down to Business

chapter thirty-two
BOND STRATEGIES

The Bare Essentials

* The *laddered portfolio* approach—which entails purchasing an equal number of bonds to mature in sequence over a chosen period of time—is one of the most effective ways to structure a portfolio of bonds. Other common approaches include *barbell* and *maturity-matching* (bullet) strategies.

* You may customize a bond portfolio to generate monthly or quarterly income.

* The *Rule of 72* is a simple way to quickly determine how many years it would take to double your money at a given yield.

There are about as many ways to structure your bond portfolio as there are stars in the sky. Poetic, eh? I've included the following approaches because they're practical (sorry, no discussion of cross-currency or derivative hedging strategies) and have proven over time to be among the most effective for fixed-income investors. That said, this chapter provides a framework: a starting point, if you will—for bond portfolios. Whatever method you choose, make sure it's customized to fit your investment objectives. And as we just discussed, keep in mind that diversification is a vital element in every investment approach.

Laddered Portfolio

Go ahead, imagine a ladder. Start at the bottom, assign each step a progressively higher maturity, and put a bond on each rung. In a nutshell, that's what the laddered portfolio approach is all about. In fact, it's so simple that you might be tempted to underestimate its value. But don't be fooled—it's one of the most effective portfolio strategies regardless of your interest rate outlook.

To construct a ladder, simply purchase an equal number of bonds to mature in sequence over a chosen period of time. The most common way is to pick a set number of years and to purchase one issue per year, but you could customize it according to your own needs. For instance, a ladder could be structured with bonds maturing once every six months or once every two years. It's up to you.

Although the length of the sequence could vary, you should ideally ladder at least five to six maturities. The types of bonds you choose should be dictated by your risk profile. For example, if you're a conservative investor with $600,000 to invest, you could construct a portfolio of Treasuries and agencies with 100 bonds maturing each year from 2007 through 2012 (see Figure 32.1).

When the first 100 bonds mature in 2007, the proceeds are reinvested after the longest maturity rung of the ladder—in this case, 2013. By con-

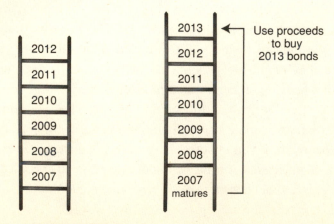

FIGURE 32.1   Laddered Portfolio

tinuing to fill the next longest slot in the ladder with the maturing proceeds, the average maturity of your portfolio remains fairly constant. Whether you reinvest in the same type of security will depend on market conditions and if your risk profile or objectives have changed. For example, if your financial circumstances have improved, you might consider picking up more yield with a Single-A corporate bond rather than reinvesting in a Triple-A security.

As promised, ladders are pretty straightforward. But why are they so effective? Because a bond ladder minimizes both reinvestment risk and interest rate risk no matter the direction of interest rates. For example, if interest rates rise, regularly maturing principal provides an opportunity to reinvest proceeds at higher yields on the longest rung of the ladder. If, instead, interest rates decline, you'd have limited reinvestment risk since only a portion of your portfolio would be exposed to the lower rate climate.

Regularly maturing bonds also provide you with money for current expenses without having to sell other financial assets that might be trading below cost basis. And laddered portfolios provide the perfect way to save for future education expenses. For instance, perhaps it's already been decided that your 3-year-old is going to medical school one day. Can you say "12 consecutive years of tuition?"

By the way, when selecting bonds for laddered portfolios, make sure they're noncallable since any early redemption would essentially defeat the purpose of the strategy. That applies to the following approaches as well.

Barbell Portfolio

Much like the laddered approach, the barbell strategy is as simple as it appears and just as easy to execute. First, let's imagine a barbell. For those of you who haven't been to the gym lately, I've provided a picture (see Figure 32.2).

Imagine that the bar represents a range of maturities, from short-term to long-term. Your bond holdings are weighted at either end of the bar,

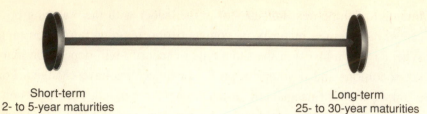

Short-term
2- to 5-year maturities

Long-term
25- to 30-year maturities

FIGURE 32.2   Barbell Portfolio

with nothing purchased in the middle. For example, bond maturities could range from 2 or 5 years on the left, and from 25 to 30 years on the right. That's a barbell. Clever, eh? You just cluster maturities at the extreme ends of the yield curve. Actually, you don't have to extend out to 30 years at the long end. You could barbell at the short end and at the intermediate term. For example, you could purchase bonds up to 2 years at the short end and in the 12- to 15-year range at the long end.

The barbell works if long-term rates decline, since longer maturities provide maximum price appreciation and allow you to lock in higher yields. If rates rose, you'd benefit from reinvesting maturing principal at higher yields. This is an appropriate strategy for institutional investors, but it's not practical for individuals. After all, your portfolio would be overweighted at the most volatile end of the curve. Frankly, I think you're better off with the laddered approach.

Maturity-Matching (Bullet) Strategy

On the surface this one's not really a strategy at all. Picture this—a bull's eye. That's a targeted maturity (get it?). Now purchase bonds in that maturity. Done. Not much to it, right? The bullet strategy makes sense when you want to be sure that a specific amount of money is available when it's absolutely required. For example, you could buy bonds that mature when a balloon payment on a mortgage is due. That's why this strategy is called maturity matching.

TABLE 32.1   Monthly and Quarterly Income Portfolios

Monthly Payments		Quarterly Payments	
Bond A	Jan, Jul	Bond A	Jan, Jul
Bond B	Feb, Aug	Bond B	Jan, Jul
Bond C	Mar, Sep	Bond C	Jan, Jul
Bond D	Apr, Oct	Bond D	Apr, Oct
Bond E	May, Nov	Bond E	Apr, Oct
Bond F	Jun, Dec	Bond F	Apr, Oct

Customizing Income

One of the most effective ways to fulfill specific income objectives is to purchase bonds with different interest payment cycles. In fact, if your primary goal is to generate income, then this strategy is for you. That's because you can design your portfolio to time the receipt of your interest payments.

Constructing a portfolio that generates monthly income is easier than you might think. Since bonds pay interest semiannually, you can buy at least six securities that pay interest in six different (twice-yearly) cycles. Or, let's say you want to supplement income to match certain fixed liabilities, such as quarterly income tax payments. You can structure a bond portfolio so that interest received coincides with the checks you'll be sending to the IRS (see Table 32.1).

This strategy, by the way, is not mutually exclusive of the laddered approach. In other words, you could simultaneously reap the benefits of a laddered strategy and have interest paid in specific months. The combined strategy is illustrated in Table 32.2.

The Rule of 72

This one's not exactly a strategy. It's more of a calculation: a tool that demonstrates the power of compounding. Essentially, the Rule of 72 is

TABLE 32.2 Integrated Laddered Portfolio with Monthly Payments

	Maturity	*Payments*
Bond A	2007	Jan, Jul
Bond B	2008	Feb, Aug
Bond C	2009	Mar, Sep
Bond D	2010	Apr, Oct
Bond E	2011	May, Nov
Bond F	2012	Jun, Dec

a simple way to quickly determine how many years it would take to double your money at a given yield. Don't worry—even if you're not a math whiz, you'll be able to handle this. Just divide 72 by the yield-to-maturity of your bond. It's that easy.

Let's flesh out an example to make sure you know how to do it. If you bought a zero coupon bond with a 6.0 percent YTM, just divide 72 by 6. That means you'd be able to double your money in 12 years if you invested in that zero today. And by the way, note that we didn't convert 6.0 percent to 0.06, if we did, it would take 1,200 years.

If you can recall some elementary algebra, you can determine the yield required to double your money for a targeted maturity. For instance, to double your principal in 15 years, you calculate yield as follows: $72 \div x = 15$. Since solving for x produces 4.8, a bond with a 4.8 percent yield would do the trick.

By the way, I've used a zero coupon bond in this example because it ensures your accrued interest is compounded at the same rate. The problem with using a coupon-paying bond is that the Rule of 72 assumes you'll reinvest all interest at the same annual rate. But, as we discussed earlier, that would be nearly impossible. So applying the Rule of 72 on those bonds is just not going to be as accurate.

chapter thirty-three

FUND STRATEGIES

The Bare Essentials

- Diversification is important since each fund has a different set of investment objectives.
- Morningstar ratings and Lipper rankings allow us to quickly assess the past performance of most available bond funds.
- *Dollar cost averaging*, or investing a specific dollar amount at periodic intervals, is one of the most effective and practical ways to invest in mutual funds.

Since mutual fund shares are inherently diversified, you may be under the impression that diversification is unnecessary. Au contraire! It's essential since, as we discussed earlier, each fund has a unique set of investment objectives. By investing in different types, you can offset risks associated with putting all your money in one sector of the market or, more importantly, depending on the performance of just one portfolio manager.

For instance, let's say you bought an aggressive bond fund containing a mix of high-yield and emerging market debt. During the following year, the high-yield sector underperformed and a large emerging market position in the fund defaulted. No wonder its NAV declined. But what if you had simultaneously invested in a government bond fund comprising

Treasuries and agencies? How would it have performed in the same scenario? In all likelihood, the problems affecting the aggressive fund would have caused a flight to quality, leading to higher demand for Triple-A securities. As a result, the government fund's NAV would rise, offsetting the underperformance of the aggressive bond fund.

There are hundreds of other ways to mix and match your fund portfolio. For example, you could offset interest rate risk by distributing your investments among funds with short-term, intermediate-term, and long-term durations. Tax-exempt investors could purchase one fund that invests in general obligation (GO) bonds and another invested in revenue securities. If you're looking for international exposure, consider Asia-Pacific or Latin American funds instead of limiting yourself to Europe.

You get the idea. Of course, as any equity mutual fund investor knows, diversification with different kinds of funds does not provide a perfect hedge against a market reversal. But it's a better strategy than suffering the consequences of one poorly timed investment. Funds managed as *core* portfolios, which diversify among bond sectors, and *balanced* funds, which also invest in stocks, do this work for you. However, you're still dependent on one portfolio manager.

Here are some key questions to think about before investing in any fund:

- Does it closely match your investment objectives?
- Is the type of fund and its strategy consistent with your risk profile?
- Does it complement other funds or bonds in your portfolio?
- How does the track record and expense ratio compare to other funds?

Using Rankings to Select a Fund

There are companies that assess mutual fund performance—sort of like the way Moody's and S&P assess bond issuers. The two leaders in this area are *Morningstar* and *Lipper*. Morningstar provides *ratings*, while Lipper provides *rankings*.

Let's start with Morningstar, which provides the most widely touted ratings in the fund business. Each fund receives up to five stars (cute, eh?) to denote its level of quality. Additionally, each is assigned a separate rating for trailing 3-, 5-, and 10-year performance records. Morningstar also provides an overall rating based on the weighted average performance. Take your pick. These ratings are printed in one-page summaries with information about expenses and fund characteristics, such as duration and investment objectives. It's also available on the web at www. morningstar.com.

Lipper, on the other hand, sorts each fund by investment objective and then ranks its performance against its peers. Many financial publications and newspapers publish Lipper rankings and use their extensive database to compile their own lists of favorite mutual funds. However, individual investors will find Morningstar information more accessible. In fact, the printed one-page summaries are available at most public libraries. And while you're at the library, take a look at those personal investment and business magazines. They regularly rank their top mutual fund picks.

Remember, though, even if you choose the best-performing five-star super-duper mutual fund, portfolio management changes or just plain old bad timing could result in poor performance. Because unlike Moody's and S&P, these are *not* forward-looking analyses. They only tell you what happened in the past. The cardinal rule, as lawyers like to say, is: *Past performance is no guarantee of future results.*

Dollar Cost Averaging

Dollar cost averaging is simply one of the most effective and practical ways to invest in mutual funds. Best of all it's easy to understand. Just determine a fixed amount you can invest at periodic intervals, say $500

TABLE 33.1   Mutual Fund Dollar Cost Averaging

Month	$ Amount	Share Price	Shares Bought
Jan	500	$10.75	46.51
Feb	500	$11.00	45.45
Mar	500	$11.25	44.44
Apr	500	$11.50	43.48
May	500	$12.12	41.25
Jun	500	$11.10	45.05
Jul	500	$11.99	41.70
Aug	500	$12.30	40.65
Sep	500	$13.00	38.46
Oct	500	$13.24	37.76
Nov	500	$13.15	38.02
Dec	500	$12.80	39.06
		$12.02	501.83
		Avg. cost/share	Total shares

a month. Then select a diversified group of funds that are appropriate to your long-term objectives. Finally, invest that fixed amount into your mutual fund portfolio each month. Now you know why this approach is sometimes called the *constant dollar plan* (see Table 33.1).

If you believe the average value of your shares will rise over time—and who doesn't?—then dollar cost averaging provides you with two benefits. First, by purchasing an equal dollar amount rather than an equal number of shares, you will have a lower average cost per share over time. More importantly, spreading out your purchases over time avoids the perils of market timing. In other words, investing $500 each month for a year entails less risk than if you invested $6,000 in one day.

chapter thirty-four

BONDS, FUNDS, OR BOTH?

The Bare Essentials

- Setting up a fully diversified bond portfolio requires a substantial financial commitment. The exact figure is debatable, but it typically ranges, at minimum, from $60,000 to $100,000.

- Low minimum investment requirements are a key advantage to mutual funds.

- If you plan to use principal to match specific liabilities, such as a down payment on a home or college tuition, individual bonds may be more appropriate.

Except for Treasuries and insured municipal bonds, most fixed-income securities carry some degree of risk. Risk, of course, is subjective depending on your personal profile and investment goals. Nevertheless, the ideal way to offset overall risk is to construct a diversified investment portfolio.

But therein lies the rub—to properly set up a fully diversified bond portfolio, you'll need to make a substantial financial commitment. Although the exact figure is debatable, it typically ranges, at minimum, from $60,000 to $100,000. That's assuming a laddered portfolio of 10 bonds in 6 to 10 different maturities. Some strategists even suggest that no more than 5 percent of your portfolio should be exposed to any one issue at a time, which would require buying at least 20 different issues. If we assume a minimum purchase of 10 bonds for each issue, that's $200,000. But what if your financial resources are more modest?

Enter mutual funds. Low minimum investment requirements are one of the key benefits of funds. However, diversification is just as important. Think about it—since every mutual fund share is equally diversified, event risk and credit risk are minimized. After all, your entire portfolio will never be dependent on the performance of a single issuer.

Then again, just because that extra million burning a hole in your pocket could be used to purchase a portfolio of individual bonds doesn't mean that it's the right strategy for you. In fact, you may be more comfortable with mutual funds; perhaps you've had success with equity funds in the past, or are partial to a specific mutual fund company. Consequently, for your purposes, a well-diversified mutual fund portfolio may be as effective as a portfolio of individual bonds.

Of course, there are disadvantages to fund investing. Since mutual fund shares lack defined maturities, principal will not be returned on a certain date. That means NAV could fall below your purchase price. Even if it rises by the time you liquidate your position, it's impossible to know exactly when that will occur. Additionally, monthly payment amounts are unpredictable, as opposed to the fixed semiannual income provided by bonds. And let's not forget, bond mutual funds are still exposed to interest rate risk.

If you plan to use principal to match specific liabilities, such as a down payment on a home or college tuition, you should purchase individual bonds. That way, regardless of a bond's performance (outside default), you could at least plan on receiving par value on a specific maturity date. For example, let's say your daughter is entering her first year of college five years from now. You could plan for that expense by purchasing bonds that mature in five years, and then in each of the subsequent three years when college tuition is due.

Structuring a portfolio of individual bonds also empowers you to be a part of every investment decision. However, it demands that you closely monitor the latest market developments. For example, an investment-grade corporate bond issuer that gets downgraded to Double-B may fall outside the boundaries of what's appropriate for your risk profile or investment objectives. What would you do?

Table 34.1 summarizes some of the most important priorities to consider when deciding to invest in a bond or a fund.

TABLE 34.1   Bonds versus Funds

Priority	Bonds	Funds
Income	Fixed (mostly)	Varies monthly
Maturity	Defined	Perpetual
Liquidity	Varies	Daily
Minimum investment	High	Low
Diversification	Requires multiple holdings	Every share is diversified
Expenses	One-time transaction charge	Ongoing annual expenses
Level of participation / control	High	Low

chapter thirty-five
PREPARING FOR CHANGING RATES

The Bare Essentials

- There are many ways to defensively position bond portfolios for both rising and declining rate environments.
- Essentially, it is prudent to shorten overall duration in your bond and mutual fund portfolios when interest rates appear likely to rise.
- Although bonds rally when rates decline, you should be prepared for heightened call, credit, and prepayment risks.

After you've finished constructing your portfolio, you could do one of two things:

1. Stick your head in the sand and hope for the best.
2. Monitor holdings for any investments that begin to deviate from your stated goals.

Choose door number 2.

A trader once told me that no matter how you feel on any given day, the train always leaves the station. In other words, the market moves ahead whether we're ready for it or not. As an investor, you don't have to go for the ride every day. But when interest rates begin to change course, your bond holdings *will* be affected.

Hopefully you've chosen one of the more flexible fixed-income strategies—like laddering—that provides sufficient diversification whether rates rise or fall. But if you haven't, or have new money to invest, there are ways to defensively position your portfolio.

Positioning for Rising Rates

Suppose economic growth starts to accelerate after an extended slowdown. Inflation pressures begin to surface, and rumblings from the Fed

TABLE 35.1 Recommendations for Rising Rates

Sell ⟶	*Buy*
Long-term maturities	Short-dated maturities, including short callable agencies and short-maturity ladders, which will provide maturing principal that can be reinvested at higher rates
Fixed-income structures that are more sensitive to rising rates, such as zero coupons	Step-up structures and adjustable/ floating-rate securities for progressively higher coupons; TIPS and I bonds to hedge against inflation
Discount bonds if you are not planning to hold them until maturity, or if you're sensitive to principal depreciation	Premium (cushion) bonds since their higher coupons equip them to withstand downward price pressures
Low-coupon preferreds	High-coupon, short callable preferreds
Low credit quality	Higher credit quality bonds since they tend to be more stable in a rising rate environment
Mortgage bonds with long average lives and interest rate–sensitive structures, such as support class and Z-class bonds	Mortgage bonds with short average lives and issues trading at a premium
Mutual funds with long average durations	Mutual funds with short average durations

indicate a tightening cycle is about to commence. What should you do? Essentially, it's time to shorten the overall duration of your portfolio. It's also time to consider corporate bonds in sectors poised to directly benefit from an economic upturn, such as transportation (vacation travel increases), industrials (more goods are produced), and retailing (consumer spending rises). See Table 35.1 for more recommendations.

Positioning for Declining Rates

When economic growth slows, interest rates decline. For the most part, this is good news for bond investors. However, credit quality, prepayment, and call risks begin to heighten. See Table 35.2 for ways to maximize return and most effectively position your portfolio for a declining rate environment.

TABLE 35.2　Recommendations for Declining Rates

To maximize:	Buy
Income	Long-duration bonds and preferreds, to lock in high coupons
Total return	Zero coupon bonds, such as STRIPS, and long-duration bonds (or funds) to maximize capital appreciation; discount mortgage-backed securities since prepays will accelerate and boost returns; extension swaps
To protect from:	
Call risk	Bullets to insure against early redemptions
Credit and default risk	Corporate bonds in defensive sectors that are more prepared to tolerate slow economic growth, such as banks, consumer products, and utilities
Prepayment risk	CMO tranches with longer lockout periods, which could slow—but not eliminate—prepayment risk

Be cautious about repositioning your entire portfolio at any one time. Investors who try to time the market this way are usually unsuccessful because it's very difficult to accurately forecast interest rate shifts. It's better to diversify, stick to a long-term plan, and make minor adjustments rather than drastic changes in an attempt to capture major market moves. The best way to do this is with the occasional bond swap, which we'll discuss in the next chapter.

chapter thirty-six
SWAPS AND TOTAL RETURN

The Bare Essentials

❦ *Bond swaps* allow us to modify holdings when the market environment or our personal objectives change. Specific rules apply when swapping for tax-loss purposes.

❦ To determine what you've *actually* earned after you've swapped or sold a bond, just calculate *total return*.

A *bond swap* simply requires selling one bond and purchasing another. Swaps make sense for a variety of reasons. For example, changes in our personal lives can cause us to modify our investment objectives. Perhaps you just had a baby (congratulations!), so it's time to consider swapping those Double-B corporate bonds for long-maturity STRIPS to coincide with Junior's college tuition payments. Or if you thought rates were about to rise, you might swap a mortgage pass-through that has a 20-year average life for the same type of security with a 4-year average life.

Other reasons to swap include:

• Increase yield, current income, or call protection
• Upgrade credit quality

- Modify maturities
- Improve tax benefits of interest income
- Enhance diversification

To determine whether a swap is worthwhile, do a side-by-side comparison of each bond. Compare coupon, credit quality, maturity, yield, and total face value. It is important to thoroughly evaluate any swap since the trade-offs may not always be immediately apparent. In fact, swapping from quality holdings to less desirable securities without fully understanding the trade-offs is one of the most common investment mistakes. In particular, be wary of giving up credit quality or liquidity simply for higher yield.

Tax-Loss Swaps

Many investors engage in *tax-loss swaps* in order to offset capital gains. As you can imagine, this strategy is especially popular in December. But, if you're thinking that you can sell the security, record the loss, and then just buy it back immediately with a lower cost basis, well, think again. There's an IRS rule known as the *30-day wash sale* to prevent you from doing just that. In effect, this rule prohibits purchasing "a substantially identical" security 30 days *before* or *after* the date of sale. So even though it's called a 30-day rule, it's actually a 61-day window.

There's a way to circumvent this rule—legally. The IRS allows you to swap your old bond for a security that is deemed to be "substantially different" from the one you sold in two of three ways—by maturity, issuer, or coupon. As a rule, if you're swapping into the same issuer, the maturity should differ by at least three years and the coupon by at least 25 basis points. For example, you could swap a 10-year Triple-A corporate bond with a 6.0 percent coupon for a 7-year, 5.75 percent coupon from the same issuer. If you're willing to sacrifice credit quality to maintain the coupon rate, you could swap into another issuer, say, a 7-year Triple-B bond at 6.0 percent. You get the idea—change two out of three, and the tax man won't come-a-knockin' at your door.

The Real Deal: Total Return

To determine what you've *actually* earned after you've swapped or sold a bond, you have to calculate total return. Just add the sale price to the interest you have generated (including any interest-on-interest), subtract that from your purchase price, and divide the whole thing by your purchase price. The equation looks like this:

$$\text{Total return} = \frac{\text{Sale price} + \text{interest (including interest-on-interest)} - \text{purchase price}}{\text{purchase price}}$$

Here's an example. Suppose you bought a hundred 20-year bonds with a 5 percent coupon at 97, and then sold them exactly three years later for 99. For the sake of simplicity, I'll ignore any interest-on-interest—let's just say you spent it. Anyway, plug in the numbers as follows:

$$\text{Total return} = \frac{\$99,000 + \$15,000 - \$97,000}{\$97,000}$$

$$= 0.175, \text{ or } 17.50\%$$

Now let's look at the same scenario, but sell the bonds at a capital loss instead, say, at 95:

$$\text{Total return} = \frac{\$95,000 + \$15,000 - \$97,000}{\$97,000}$$

$$= 0.134, \text{ or } 13.40\%$$

That's not bad, considering you sold the bonds below your cost basis.

I didn't include any transaction costs in the preceding calculations since, as we will soon discuss, they are usually embedded in the price. However, if you pay a commission, subtract those costs from the sale price first. Of course, there is one important factor that's not in these calculations: taxes incurred on interest and capital gains. But I'll leave that up to your accountant.

chapter thirty-seven
WHAT NOT TO DO

The Bare Essentials

🍀 The most common investment mistakes include: reaching for yield, acting like a trader, refusing to purchase premium bonds, and overweighting a single asset class.

Nobody's perfect. Well, my mother thinks I am, but I keep telling her that it just isn't true. Experienced investors understand that mistakes inevitably occur, no matter how many precautions are taken. The following are some of the most common investment mistakes that I've observed.

Reaching for Yield

Just as stock investors can be blinded by their desire to maximize capital appreciation, bond investors can be blinded by their desire to maximize yield. Some call it greed, but I think it's human nature—we naturally attempt to make the most of our financial resources.

The decision to ignore underlying fundamentals in exchange for higher yields can exact a heavy toll. Of course, it's tempting to ignore any doubts and believe that somehow we've spotted an opportunity.

But that's how investors get into trouble. In fact, higher-than-average yields usually signal more risk than meets the eye. For example, on the surface a Triple-B corporate bond offering 300 basis points more than comparable securities may appear to be a great value. However, it's likely on its way to junk status. Remember, the market is a *leading* indicator. As a rule, issuers whose bonds trade with much higher yields than their peers reflect deteriorating fundamentals. It might be cliché, but don't forget that old saying, "If it looks too good to be true, it probably is."

Investors commonly reach for yield after interest rates have declined. That's when investors experience *rate shock*, which is the tendency to look where rates have been instead of where they're going. This often leads us to consider investments that stretch or exceed our customary risk parameters. For example, let's say rates declined. If you are a conservative investor whose agencies were called, you might be tempted to purchase junk bonds to compensate for lower yields. Before you purchase that marginal security, calculate the additional annual income that it would generate. Nine times out of 10 you'll discover that it's insignificant and hardly worth the elevated risk.

Acting Like a Trader

Are you an investor or a trader? Here's a hint—how many times did you hear "day trader" before the stock market bubble burst in 2000? And how many times have you heard it since? As the saying goes, "Don't confuse a bull market with brilliance." So don't allow yourself to fall into a shortsighted trap. Although we all fantasize about making quick profits, it's also the fastest route to the doghouse. Where's that Warren Buffett fellow to back me up?

Even if you consider short-term trading to be a skill, you'd be hard-pressed to apply it to the fixed-income market. There are two reasons for this: pricing and timing. Let's start with pricing. Unless you're transacting directly with broker-dealers from your home trading terminal for $10 million at a clip, it's going to be difficult to profit from short-term price swings in the bond market.

Market timing is a dangerous game—even the best market professionals fall victim to it. Remember the Long Term Capital Management hedge fund that nearly brought down the world's financial markets in 1998? That firm employed two Nobel Prize–winning economists and the most skilled bond traders on Wall Street. Of course, market patterns tend to move in cycles—even the Long Term Capital investments eventually became profitable (unfortunately, it was months after the company was dissolved). So, go figure—their timing was all wrong. It reflects an old truism: The market has the ability to remain irrational longer than most investors have the ability to remain solvent.

Refusing to Purchase Premium Bonds

Many investors make the mistake of equating premium bonds with overpaying for a security. After all, since the bond is going to be repaid at par, doesn't that mean you're automatically in the red? No, it doesn't, because higher coupons usually compensate for the cost of the premium. And don't forget, these securities will be more resilient than other bonds if rates rise. Since many investors are not cognizant of these benefits, premium bonds sometimes present better values than comparable fixed-income securities trading at a discount.

Overweighting a Single Asset Class

After the technology bubble burst in 2000, diversification (or more accurately the lack of it) was a hot topic. Seems an overwhelming number of investors were heavily invested in that sector. The pain, however, was not limited to stock investors—soon afterwards, many corporate bond investors saw some of their investments falter. It was a harsh lesson, but one that clearly illustrates why diversification is crucial. The old adage rings true: don't put all your eggs in one basket.

More Common Mistakes

- Purchasing securities before establishing objectives
- Investing without understanding the risks
- Failing to read the prospectus
- Investing on your own even though you're not prepared or willing to monitor your portfolio
- Swapping bonds without being fully aware of the trade-offs

chapter thirty-eight

PRACTICAL MATTERS

The Bare Essentials

- Since the bond market is largely traded over-the-counter, fixed-income investors must be flexible.

- *Markups* and *markdowns* are to bond investors what commissions are to stock investors; they're the cost of doing business each time a transaction occurs.

- Capital gains and losses generated by bonds and stocks are accorded similar treatment by the U.S. tax code.

In the bond market, the key word to remember is flexibility. Don't get me wrong—that doesn't mean compromising your standards or altering your objectives. I'm just suggesting that having a generic set of objectives is more productive than merely setting your sights on a specific bond issue, because, unlike stocks, that bond might not be available unless someone has decided to sell it.

For example, let's say you're looking for a six-year noncallable General Electric issue, but your financial advisor informs you that it is not in the firm's inventory. Knowing that availability varies from dealer to dealer, you inquire at several other investment firms. Still no luck. You search online. Nothing. Instead of tearing your hair out, evaluate why you wanted to buy it—large industrial company, Triple-A credit quality, six years to maturity. Then search for bonds with similar characteristics.

New bond offerings operate a little differently than the secondary market. You place an *indication of interest* with a bond dealer and, depending on demand, your request will be either fully or partially filled. However, just like stock IPOs, you could get *shut out* completely. Of course, this does not apply to Treasury auctions or corporate medium-term notes (MTNs), which are offered on a weekly basis. (Since MTNs are sparsely traded, they are meant for buy-and-hold investors only.)

Whether you're buying or selling, keep in mind what we discussed about the inefficiency of bond pricing. For instance, the only way to accurately assess a bond's current market value is to request a bid from a broker. Furthermore, it's entirely probable three different broker-dealers could provide three different bids, especially if it's an illiquid security. Don't forget, there's no New York Bond Exchange.

These pricing issues are common because individual investors transact infrequently and for much smaller amounts than institutions. Now $50,000 to $100,000 might sound like a lot of money to you, but it's insignificant compared to institutional investors who trade in the tens of millions. After all, if you were a bond trader whose livelihood depended on transaction volume, wouldn't you prefer to move larger amounts of inventory in fewer trades?

This is not meant to dissuade you from buying bonds: it's just the reality of the fixed-income market. There is good news, though—since traders don't like to hold onto small blocks of bonds, it's often where you can identify value.

Moral of the story: If you're going to purchase individual bonds, muster the commitment to be a buy-and-hold investor. Because unless your portfolio is limited to Treasuries or agencies, selling small blocks of bonds is just not a prudent course of action.

Transaction Costs

Whether you're quoted a bid or an offer, the net price always incorporates a *markup* or a *markdown*. Markups (and markdowns) are to bond investors what commissions are to stock investors—they're the cost of doing business every time a *principal* transaction occurs—or when an investment firm buys and sells for its own account. Broker-dealers also act as *agents* when they purchase or sell bonds outside their own inventory or on an exchange. In that case, you'll pay a commission.

Markups occur when a bond is purchased, and markdowns occur when they're sold. Think of it this way; when you sell a bond, the transaction cost causes a bid to be *marked down*. Conversely, when you purchase a bond, the transaction cost causes the offer price to be *marked up*. For example, a bond that cost 101 could be marked up 1 point and sold to you at a 102 offer. Conversely, if you were quoted a 101 bid, it could reflect a 102 base price with a 1-point markdown.

Unlike commissions, markups and markdowns are embedded into the transaction price. As a result, it won't be clear how much you've been charged. These costs typically range from as little as 0.125 to 4.0 percent of the total purchase price. Frequently traded bonds, such as Treasuries, incur the lowest transaction costs, while long-dated, low-quality, and illiquid issues, as well as small orders, generally incur the highest.

You'll receive a *confirmation* whenever you buy or sell a security. The day of the transaction is called the *trade date*, and the day money is due is called the *settlement date*. Treasuries and mutual funds settle on the next business day, while all other bonds usually settle *regular way*, or in three business days. Sometimes you can arrange a *next-day settlement* for bonds that settle regular way. Don't forget to account for accrued interest whenever you purchase or sell a bond.

Capital Gains and Losses

With rare exceptions, capital gains or losses occur when a bond is sold prior to its stated maturity. At risk of stating the obvious, a loss occurs whenever a security is sold below its purchase price (or *cost basis*), and a gain occurs when it's sold above. Capital gains and losses generated by bonds and stocks are accorded equal treatment by the U.S. tax code. So if you're a stock investor, this should be pretty familiar.

Any security bought and sold within 12 months is considered a short-term capital gain and taxed at your nominal income tax rate. Beyond 12 months, capital gains are considered long-term and taxed at a maximum

15 percent rate. You can use gains and losses incurred by fixed-income transactions to offset those in equities. Interest income, by the way, is taxed as ordinary income, although some dividend-paying preferred stock now qualifies for the lower 15 percent rate.

You are not required to pay capital gains tax when you purchase a new issue that is priced at a discount and held to maturity. This is known as an *original issue discount* (OID), which allows you to recognize the gain as ordinary income along with interest payments.

Since mutual funds are actively managed, they produce capital gains that are distributed at least once each year. You'll be responsible for paying taxes on these gains in the calendar year that they're received. That means if you purchase a fund just before one of these distributions (often in December), you'll be faced with a tax bill for gains you didn't even enjoy. So be sure to inquire about when a fund is going to make these distributions before you invest.

WRAPPING UP

As the book goes to print, Treasury yields are hovering near 50-year lows and the bond market has outperformed the stock market for three consecutive years.

Meanwhile, world events continue to heighten anxiety about the sustainability of a global economic recovery. From the residual terrorism fears that began on September 11, 2001, to the wars in Afghanistan and Iraq, to panic that erupted over the SARS epidemic, uncertainty now appears to be a fixture in our lives, one that may not meaningfully recede for some time to come.

In the midst of this secular shift, the bond market has presented a sort of oasis for many investors. Although it has had its share of volatility, for the most part it has anchored investors to something predictable and sound. And, it has certainly helped to cushion the devastating blow the equity market delivered to investment portfolios during the first few years of the millennium.

After such a strong run by the bond market, odds are that stocks will soon reclaim the limelight. That's alright, because nothing can dilute the complementary strengths that bonds provide to a diversified portfolio. And besides, no matter what happens in the bond market, you are now well prepared to map your own route to investment success.

GLOSSARY

Accrued interest: amount of interest accumulated, but not yet paid, between semi-annual payment dates.

Adjustable rate preferreds: perpetual securities with a variable, rather than fixed, quarterly dividend that floats between an upper and lower range, or collar.

Agency securities: issued by U.S. Federal agencies and privately run corporations known as *government-sponsored enterprises* (*GSE*s) to provide funding for a specific public purpose.

Agency transaction: when a broker-dealer purchases or sells a bond outside its own inventory or on an exchange.

Alternative minimum tax (AMT): targets wealthy investors; applied to the interest generated by some municipal bonds by adding tax-preference items back to adjusted gross income.

Anticipation notes: short-term securities issued by municipalities to bridge financing gaps until revenue is received. Most mature in less than one year, and are commonly issued as: tax anticipation notes (TANs), revenue anticipation notes (RANs), tax and revenue anticipation notes (TRANs), and bond anticipation notes (BANs).

Ask: *see* Offer.

Asset allocation: the process of segmenting a portfolio into different types of investments.

Asset-backed securities: structured like mortgage bonds, except they're backed by receivables from assets other than real estate—such as credit card loans, airplane leases and auto loans.

Baby bonds: debt preferreds created by broker-dealers from their own inventory by splitting large blocks of $1,000 par bonds into $25 increments.

Banker's acceptance (BA): one- to six-month money market instrument sold at a discount; typically used by importers and exporters.

Barbell portfolio: strategy whereby bond holdings are concentrated among the shortest and longest maturities with nothing purchased in between.

Basis point (bp): represents 1/100th of a percent (100 basis points equals one percent).

Bearer bonds: these were physical certificates with actual coupons that bond investors would clip and mail to the issuer's trustee in exchange for earned interest. Distribution of these bonds was suspended in 1982; today all bonds are issued in electronic (book entry) form.

Bid: price at which a bond is sold; the bid is always lower than the offer.

Bond: a security that pays a specified rate of interest for a limited amount of time and returns principal on a defined date.

Bond equivalent yield (BEY): used in order to accurately compare Treasury bills to the annualized yield of a coupon-bearing security; typically quoted with the discount rate.

Bond swap: selling one bond with the intent of using the proceeds to purchase another.

Book entry form: electronic record of ownership reflected on a bank or brokerage statement. Interest payments are distributed directly by mail or deposited into investment accounts.

Broker-dealers: investment firms that broker (sell) and deal (issue) bonds.

Bullet securities (bullets): bonds devoid of any early redemption features.

Bullet strategy: *see* Maturity matching.

Busted convert: when the stock price is well below a convertible bond's conversion price; the option becomes worthless and the security's price only reflects the intrinsic value of the bond.

Call: early redemption feature of a bond.

Call protection: a certain number of years during which the issuer does not have the right to call a bond.

Call risk: holder of a callable bond runs the risk of the bond being redeemed prior to maturity.

Call schedule: the series of early redemption dates for a callable bond.

Callable bond: feature that grants the issuer the right to retire a bond prior to its maturity, beginning on a specific date.

Capital gain: when a security is sold above its purchase price; considered a short-term gain if sold within 12 months of purchase and taxed at nominal income tax rate; beyond 12 months is long-term and taxed at a maximum 15 percent rate.

Capital loss: when a security is sold below the purchase price.

Capital preservation: investment goal that seeks to minimize principal risk.

Capital structure: ranks debt and equity according to the claim they have on a company's assets.

Cash management bill: short-term security auctioned by the U.S. Treasury to supplement the financing provided by T-bills.

Certificate of deposit (CD): time deposit that has the qualities of a bond but is not an SEC-registered offering; typically insured by the Federal Deposit Insurance Corporation (FDIC) for up to $100,000 (principal and interest combined).

Closed-end fund: actively managed bond fund with a fixed number of shares that trades with a bid/ask spread on a stock exchange or in the over-the-counter market.

Collateralized mortgage obligation (CMO): a group of pass-through securities carved into different classes (tranches); on average, CMOs contain 60 to 100 different tranches.

Commercial paper (CP): short-term debt issued by large corporations; matures in 270 days or less.

Competitive bid: indicates desired purchase amount and yield at U.S. Treasury auction.

Compound interest: computed on the original principal as well as accumulated earned interest.

Confirmation: receipt sent to investors outlining details of a transaction whenever a security is bought or sold.

Consumer Price Index (CPI): the most widely watched consumer inflation barometer, expressed as a percentage of year-over-year growth.

Contrarian investor: one who makes investment decisions that disagree with consensus.

Conversion parity: when a convertible bond's price is equal to the current market value of the common stock to be received if converted.

Conversion price: the price a convertible security may be exchanged for common stock.

Conversion ratio: a convertible bond's par value divided by its conversion price.

Convertible security (convert): a bond or preferred with an option that allows for an exchange of the security for common stock of the same issuer at a specified price.

Corporate bonds (corporates): securities issued by the private sector which are used for a variety of purposes, from working capital, to building factories or acquiring other companies.

Cost basis: the net purchase price of a security.

Covenants: legal protections provided to investors as contained in the indenture.

Coupon: a bond's stated annual interest rate.

Credit rating: quantifies risk by providing a forward-looking analysis of an issuer's ability to make timely interest payments and return principal at maturity.

Credit rating agencies: independent companies paid by bond issuers to evaluate their financial profiles and provide rankings; sanctioned and closely monitored by the SEC, the three major agencies are Moody's Investors Service (Moody's), Standard & Poors (S&P) and Fitch Ratings.

Cumulative dividend: if preferred dividends are suspended, then missed payments accumulate; the cumulative dividend must be repaid to investors if dividends are resumed.

Currency risk: the potential of another currency to appreciate or depreciate in value when converted back to one's home currency.

Current yield: a bond's annual rate of return determined by multiplying the coupon by par value, dividing it by the purchase price and multiplying by 100; this yield does not incorporate future interest payments or the difference between purchase price and redemption value.

Curtailment: when homeowners pay more than the monthly amount that's due, it's applied directly to mortgage principal.

Cushion bonds: *see* Premium bonds.

CUSIP (Committee on Uniform Securities Identification Procedures): a unique nine-digit (alphanumeric) number assigned to each bond.

Death put: *see* Survivors option.

Debenture: bond backed by an issuer's general credit standing rather than by specific assets.

Debt market: more commonly known as the bond market.

Default: when an issuer fails to meet its financial obligations; usually followed by bankruptcy.

Deflation: when consumer prices decline over a long period of time; opposite of inflation.

Diluting shareholder equity: when companies increase stock issuance, the percentage of the company that is owned by current shareholders is reduced.

Discount: when a bond's price trades below its $1,000 par value.

Discount notes (discos): zero coupon agency securities issued at a discount to par with up to one-year of maturity.

Distressed market: where professional "vulture" investors place bets among troubled or defaulted issuers.

Dividend Received Deduction (DRD) preferreds: 70% of the dividend generated by these securities is a tax break to certain corporate investors that hold them for at least 46 days.

Diversification: a strategy that seeks to improve the overall rate of return and substantially reduce risk if a portfolio is populated with a number of uncorrelated investments.

Dollar cost average: a fixed amount invested at periodic intervals; usually applied to mutual fund investing; also known as the *constant dollar plan*.

Downgrade: when a credit agency lowers the rating of an issuer, typically when its financial condition deteriorates.

Duration: a measure of the sensitivity of a bond's price to interest rate fluctuations; represents the percentage change in a bond's price given a 1% rise or fall in interest rates.

Dutch (single-price) auction: a Treasury auction whereby all investors receive the same yield for their bids.

Easing: if the Federal Open Market Committee (FOMC) concludes that the economy needs stimulus, the funds rate is lowered; also known as "accommodative" monetary policy.

Emerging market bonds: issued by companies and governments from evolving market-based economies; issuers are typically located in Latin America, Eastern Europe and Southeast Asia.

Equity market: more commonly known as the stock market.

Event risk: risk related to potential events that would affect the credit quality of a bond, such as a takeover, political or economic upheavals.

Expense ratio: derived from annual expense fees charged in order to cover a fund's overhead; calculated by dividing total expenses by total assets in the fund.

Extension risk: when rates rise, mortgage bond prepayments slow and more principal remains in the loan pool for a longer period of time; consequently, average life lengthens.

Face value: *see* Par value.

Fallen angel: an issuer downgraded from investment-grade to high-yield.

Federal funds rate (fed funds rate): the interest rate that banks charge each other for overnight loans to meet reserve requirements; its target is determined eight times a year by the Federal Open Market Committee (FOMC).

Flight to quality: when risk aversion heightens due to political, economic or market risk, strong inflows to the safest investments (such as Treasuries) occur.

Future value: what money today would be worth at some point in the future, assuming a specified rate of return.

General Obligation (GO) bond: issued by municipalities that have the ability to tax constituents; state governments dominate this type of issuance.

Global bonds: often refers to bonds simultaneously issued in different currencies; typically denominated in U.S. dollar, UK sterling and/or euro currencies.

Government-sponsored enterprises (GSEs): U.S. federally-designated companies affiliated with, but separate from, the U.S. government; major issuers of agency and mortgage bonds.

High-grade bonds: *see* Investment-grade bonds.

High-yield (junk) bonds: speculative issuers rated below investment-grade by the credit agencies. Bonds are ranked from "Ba1" to "C" by Moody's and from "BB+" to "D" by S&P and Fitch.

Illiquidity: *see* Liquidity.

Indenture: a formal, legally binding contract that bond issuers are required to publish; comprehensively describes specific terms and conditions of a bond offering and contains provisions meant to protect both parties.

Indication of interest: investor submits desired purchase amount to broker-dealer for new bond offering.

Inflation: when the cost of a product or service rises and quality remains the same; also, when spending increases relative to supply—think of it as too much money chasing too few goods.

Insured bonds: municipal bonds (and sometimes taxable issuers) backed by insurance which guarantees that interest and principal will be paid should the issuer default; automatically receive Triple-A ratings by credit agencies.

Interest expense: interest paid to bondholders that provide corporations with a pretax deduction.

Interest-on-interest: reinvesting interest payments and earning interest on that new principal.

Interest rate risk: the effect of fluctuating interest rates on bond prices.

Intermediate-term bonds: bonds with 5- to 12-years until maturity.

Inverted yield curve: when short-term rates are higher than intermediate and long-term rates; usually occurs when the Federal Reserve tightens the funds rate in order to slow down a fast-growing economy and creeping inflation pressures.

Investment-grade (high-grade) bonds: comprises issuers that are deemed to be in good financial health and are unlikely to have trouble meeting their debt obligations. Bonds are ranked from Triple-A (highest) to Triple-B (lowest).

Jumbo CDs: certificates of deposit sold in multiples of $100,000.

Junk bonds: *see* high-yield bonds.

Laddered portfolio strategy: investors purchase an equal number of bonds to mature in sequence over a chosen period of time.

Leverage: an issuer's overall debt level relative to its current cash flow or total capital; non–investment-grade companies are considerably leveraged.

Liquidity: the market's demand for (and supply of) a particular security. When a bond is said to have good liquidity, it can be readily converted into cash near the price that it was last bought or sold. Opposite: *illiquidity*.

Load: an upfront or back-end sales charge on a mutual fund.

Lockout: the period prior to the first principal payment of certain collateralized mortgage obligations; monthly cash flow consists of interest only.

Long-term bonds: bonds with maturities that exceed twelve years.

Maturity matching (Bullet strategy): purchasing bonds in a targeted maturity to ensure that a specific amount of money is available on a specific date.

Managed accounts: usually require a minimum investment of $100,000 to $250,000, which is either turned over to a professional money manager or allocated among several different portfolio managers to match a strategy aligned with stated investment objectives.

Markups and Markdowns: analogous to stock commissions, they're the cost of doing business every time a principal transaction occurs. The net bid or offer incorporates this charge. Markups occur when a bond is purchased, and markdowns occur when a bond is sold.

Maturity: a bond's predetermined lifespan at issuance.

Maturity date: when a bond's final interest payment and principal are distributed, effectively terminating the obligation of the borrower (issuer) to the lender (investor).

Medium-term note (MTN): senior unsecured debt with a survivor option feature that differs from typical corporate bonds due to its ability to generate quarterly or monthly payments; also structured as 2- to 5-year bullets and as 10- and 15-year callable securities.

Money market funds: mutual funds invested in short-term securities, such as Treasury bills, CDs, banker's acceptance, and commercial paper; provide a higher rate of return than savings accounts, can offer check-writing privileges and are readily available as cash.

Money market securities: short-term instruments that mature in one year or less, such as Treasury bills, CDs, banker's acceptance, and commercial paper.

Mortgage-backed securities (MBS): bonds secured by real estate; most mortgage bonds are backed by residential mortgages, although some are commercial-backed securities.

Mortgage pool: created when a group of mortgage loans with similar interest rate and maturity characteristics are packaged together.

Municipal bonds: issued by state and local governments to finance projects that serve the public interest; popular with individual investors due to their tax-free interest income.

Negative convexity: a feature typically associated with mortgage bonds whereby prices tend to decline more than other bonds when interest rates rise, and appreciate less when rates decline.

Negative slope: *see* Inverted yield curve.

Net asset value (NAV): a fund's total value less expenses then divided by the number of outstanding shares. The current NAV is determined at the end of each business day.

No-load funds: funds that do not have an upfront or back-end sales charge.

Nominal yield: a bond's coupon rate; also the prevailing interest rate without incorporating inflation.

Noncompetitive bid: investors submit this in a Treasury auction, which specifies how many bonds desired to purchase; all noncompetitive requests are filled.

Noncumulative dividends: allow issuers to resume regular payments without compensating investors for lost dividends.

Nongovernmental purpose bonds: tax-exempt securities used to fund initiatives that more narrowly serve the public interest or are associated with the private sector.

Odd lot: in the bond market, anything less than a round lot (at least one million dollars par value).

Offer (Ask): the price at which an investor may purchase a bond; always higher than the bid.

On-the-run Treasury: the most recently auctioned benchmark Treasury securities; older securities are considered off-the-run.

Open-end mutual funds: actively managed bond funds that issue an unlimited number of shares; not traded on an exchange but instead bought and sold by the fund company itself.

Original issue discount (OID): when a new issue is purchased at a discount and held to maturity, investors can recognize the gain as ordinary income instead of capital gain.

Outstanding securities: secondary market bonds that have been issued but have not yet matured or been called.

Over-the-counter (OTC): a "virtual" market where the bulk of the bond market's daily trading volume is transacted. Bond traders buy and sell directly with each other, not through a specialist on an organized exchange.

Par value: also known as face value; the dollar amount received at maturity and the value used to calculate interest; bonds are customarily issued with a $1,000 par value.

Pass-through securities (pass-throughs): conduits whereby mortgage payments are collected in a pool and distributed to bond investors through a trust that is created at issuance.

Patriot Bonds: *see* Series EE Savings Bonds.

Phantom income: interest generated by zero coupon bonds; accrued interest from most zero bonds is taxed as if you had actually received it that year.

Planned Amortization Class (PAC) bonds: type of mortgage bond that has cash flow allocated to each tranche based on a schedule with preset limits for prepayments so average life and yield are relatively stable.

Poison put: featured in high yield issues, it allows bonds to be redeemed at a slight premium if there's a "change of control," such as a company buyout.

Portfolio managers: mutual fund and closed-end funds are actively managed by these investment professionals.

Positive slope: yields increase as maturities lengthen. A positive slope is considered "normal" because uncertainty naturally accelerates as money is invested for longer periods of time.

Premium: when a bond's price trades above its $1,000 par value.

Premium (cushion) bonds: these securities trade above par value; higher coupon rates "cushion" the downward pressure on bond prices.

Prepayments (prepays): unscheduled mortgage bond principal payments; since most homeowners do not adhere to a specific payment schedule, monthly cash flow generated by mortgage bonds varies over time.

Prepayment risk: associated with the rise in prepays due to higher refinancing activity, causing the amount of principal returned to the investor to be larger than expected.

Prepayment speeds: traders determine the pace that principal is returned to investors using historical data and then utilize it to price mortgage-backed securities.

Pre-refunded bonds (pre-re's): callable municipal bonds that have been refinanced; issuers then distribute refunding bonds at lower interest rates and purchase Treasuries with the proceeds.

Price transparency: when the price and cost of a transaction are fully disclosed.

Primary dealers: a select group of 22 investment firms and banks that are key participants in the Treasury auction process.

Primary market: where new bonds are issued; also known as "syndicate."

Principal transaction: when an investment firm buys and sells for its own account.

Private sector: comprises domestic and multinational corporations that issue bonds as an alternative to bank loans and stock offerings.

Prospectus: issuers are required to publish this document that outlines the key provisions of a new offering. It summarizes crucial information from the indenture and is distributed to prospective buyers; includes use of proceeds, description of the issuer, and risk factors.

Preferred securities (preferreds): securities with characteristics that uniquely straddle the debt and equity markets; were issued as nonvoting shares of stock, but today they're more commonly issued as debt; typically have a $25 par value, fixed quarterly payments, at least 30 years to maturity and five years of call protection.

Preferred stock: perpetual security that declares dividends instead of paying interest; senior to common stock—but subordinate to bonds.

Present value: the amount that a sum of money in the future is worth today, assuming a specified rate of return.

Private activity bonds: issued by municipalities but are associated with projects that are not government-run; may be taxable, depending on the extent to which they benefit public interests.

Private label pass-throughs: pass-throughs that are created by financial institutions and are usually rated Triple-A or Double-A; not created by government agencies.

Private placements: mostly high-yield bonds sold directly to qualified institutional buyers (QIBs) rather than through a public offering; subject to an SEC regulation known as Rule 144A.

Public purpose bonds: are issued directly by state or local authorities for projects typically financed by governments; including construction of public schools, sanitation facilities, water treatment plants and highway improvements. Public purpose bonds are exempt from federal, state and local taxes.

Public Securities Association (PSA) standard (also known as **prepayment speed assumption**): assumes new mortgage loans are less likely to be prepaid than older ones; used to determine mortgage bond prices.

Pro-rata sinker: stipulates an equal percentage of bonds to be redeemed will be spread among all investors, instead of by lottery like other sinkers.

Public sector: comprises federal debt issues known as Treasuries, and state and local government issues known as municipals.

Put bond: provides investors with the option to put a bond back to the issuer on specific dates. If a putable bond is trading below par on its put date, it may be redeemed at par.

Rate shock: after interest rates have substantially declined, investors tend to look where rates have been instead of where they are going; often leads to common mistake known as "reaching for yield."

Reaching for yield: common mistake made by bond investors whereby risk factors are ignored due to the desire to maximize yield.

Real interest rate: nominal yield minus the inflation rate, which represents the net increase of spending power above and beyond the eroding effects of inflation.

Real estate investment trust (REIT) preferred: preferred stock issued by companies that manage property or real estate loans.

Real estate mortgage investment conduit (REMIC): see collateralized mortgage obligation.

Recovery value: the amount a bond is worth after interest payments have been halted and the issuer defaults.

Refinancing (prepayment) wave: when rates drop dramatically in a short period of time, many homeowners tend to refinance concurrently.

Refunding announcement: provides investors with details about the amount of Treasury supply to expect in the upcoming quarter.

Regular way: an investment that settles in three business days.

Reinvestment risk: when a bond is called, investors are usually faced with the less attractive option of reinvesting the proceeds at a lower rate.

Reopening: the Treasury department issues new debt by adding to older issues instead of holding an auction.

Repurchase agreements (repos): money market instruments where an investor arranges to sell securities, but agrees to buy them back (usually overnight) at a specific price.

Revenue bonds: bonds that are backed by revenue and fees collected by the facility that's being funded. Debt service for these bonds is directly supported by the income generated by the project.

Risk profile: classifying an investor according to the ability to withstand market volatility and overall risk; typically: conservative, moderate, aggressive and speculative.

Round lot: in the bond market, not less than one million dollars in par value.

Rule of 72: a method of determining the years required to double your money at a given yield; calculated by dividing 72 by the yield-to-maturity.

Savings bonds: bonds issued with the same "full faith and credit" government guarantee as Treasuries, but are non-marketable securities and are not traded in the secondary market. The three types of savings bonds are: Series EE, Series HH/H and Series I.

SEC mutual fund cost calculator: a quick and easy way to estimate and compare bond fund expenses. Can be found at www.sec.gov.

Secondary market: where outstanding bonds are bought and sold.

Separate Trading of Registered Interest and Principal of Securities (STRIPS): zero coupon Treasury bond that is purchased at a deep discount to face value; created by broker-dealers and are not auctioned.

Sequential bonds: has separate tranches with principal that pays off sequentially; the average life of each preceding tranche becomes shorter than the last.

Serial bonds: large new bond issues that feature several different maturities.

Series EE savings bond: interest is pegged to Treasuries and sold at 50% of face value. (See Savings bonds.)

Series HH/H: structured just like traditional interest-paying bonds; scheduled to be discontinued in 2004. (See Savings bonds.)

Series I savings bond: an inflation-indexed savings bond whose value is pegged to the Consumer Price Index for Urban Consumers (or CPI-U); sold at face value. (See Savings bonds.)

Settlement date: the day money is due for an investment.

SEC yield: a standard calculation that mutual funds must disclose to investors in order to ensure that the investment may be fairly assessed compared to its peers.

Short coupon: when the first interest payment is not a full six months because the semiannual coupon payment dates are dictated by maturity, not the issuance date.

Short-term bonds: bonds with 1- to 5-year maturities.

Simple interest: straight payment of interest that is not compounded.

Sinking fund securities (sinkers): securities with early redemption features that designate a specific number of bonds to be redeemed on a periodic basis before final maturity; bonds selected for redemption are usually determined by lottery.

Sovereign risk: encompasses uncertainties associated with investing in another country.

Split rating: when rating agencies assign different ratings to the same issue; rarely exceeds more than one or two notches.

Spread: difference between the bid and the offer price is the bid/offer spread; the difference between two bond yields is know as the yield spread.

Step-up note (step-up): Fannie Mae, Freddie Mac, and some corporations issue these securities with maturities that typically do not exceed 15 years, are callable, and have coupon rates that increase according to a preset schedule over time.

Support bonds: bonds that absorb prepayments from PAC tranches and compensate those securities for any shortfall in principal payments.

Supranational bonds: U.S. dollar–denominated international securities formed to promote economic development and are backed by the federal governments of at least two countries.

Survivor's option (death put): most MTNs retain this feature which allows heirs to redeem bonds at par should the registered owner of the bond die, even if it's trading at a steep discount.

Syndicate: a group of investment firms organized by the underwriter to help market a new bond issue to prospective buyers.

Taxable equivalent yield (TEY): a calculation investors use to level the playing field when comparing taxable bond yields to tax-exempt (municipal) yields.

Tax-exempt money market funds: funds that invest in short-term Treasury and municipal debt. There are two types: federally-tax exempt, and state funds that provide state and local exemptions.

Term bonds: bond issues offered with only one maturity date.

30-day wash sale: this rule prohibits purchasing a "substantially identical" security thirty days before or after the date of sale.

Throwaway bid: a below-market bid for a bond usually due to its illiquidity.

Tightening: when the Federal Reserve raises the fed funds rate to slow economic activity; also known as tight monetary policy.

Total return: accurately measures what you really earned on a bond; calculated by adding the sale price to the interest generated (including any interest-on-interest), subtract that from the purchase price, and divide the whole thing by the purchase price.

Trade flat: securities bought and sold without accrued interest, like preferred stock.

Treasury auctions: regularly scheduled sales of Treasury securities.

Treasury bills (T-bills): direct obligations of the U.S. government with maturities of four weeks, three months and six months. These are zero coupons sold at a discount to face value.

Treasury bonds: direct obligations of the U.S. government issued with maturities over 10 years, up to 30 years. Auctions of these securities are currently suspended.

Treasury inflation protected securities (TIPS): issued with 10- and 30-year maturities, these inflation-indexed bonds are designed to benefit from rising inflation. Principal is adjusted daily by a factor tied to the performance of the Consumer Price Index-Urban Consumers (CPI-U).

Treasury notes: direct obligations of the U.S. government issued with maturities of two to 10 years; they pay interest semiannually at a fixed rate of interest.

Trust preferred: subordinated debt placed into a trust, which then issues $25 par securities (some trade in the corporate market at $1,000 face value). Quarterly interest is generated by debt securities held in the trust.

Treasury securities: bonds that are direct obligations of the U.S. government.

Treasury yield curve: plots the yield-to-maturity of all on-the-run Treasury securities—from 3- and 6-month bills, to 2-, 3-, 5-, and 10-year notes, plus the 30-year bond.

Trustee: bank appointed by a bond issuer to administer interest payments to investors.

12b1 fees: what funds charge to pay for promotional and general marketing expenses.

Underwriter: an investment bank that arranges a bond sale on behalf of an issuer; advises issuer on the timing and terms of the offering, such as the amount of bonds to issue and the coupon rate.

Unit investment trusts (UITs): a fixed group of bonds held in a trust that is not actively managed. Since there is no active secondary market for UITs, shares must be sold directly back to the issuer.

Upgrade: rating action that occurs when an issuer's financial security strengthens.

Weighted average life: the estimated number of years when half a mortgage pool's principal will be returned to the investor.

Whole loan: non-agency CMO that is created by financial institutions in the private sector—such as investment banks—and is the sole obligation of those issuers.

Window: estimated time frame between the first and last principal payments of a CMO tranche.

Yankee securities: non-U.S. incorporated companies that issue dollar-denominated debt in the United States; these issuers tend to be quasi-government monopolies or privatized companies.

Yield-to-call (YTC): the same calculation as YTM, except it targets a call date instead of the maturity date. YTC incorporates the future stream of reinvested coupon payments, the price paid for the bond, as well as the price received at each early redemption date.

Yield-to-maturity (YTM): the percentage rate of return assuming a bond is held until maturity and interest payments are reinvested at the same nominal yield. YTM integrates any difference between par value and the actual price paid.

Yield-to-worst (YTW): the lowest yield received: it's the lower of a bond's YTM and YTC. This is the most conservative way to view a bond's potential return and should always be assessed when purchasing any callable security.

Zero coupon bonds (accrual bonds): bonds that do not make cash interest payments to investors. Instead of receiving a payment every six months, earned interest accrues to the face value of the bond until it matures at $1,000 par value. Zeros are issued at a deep discount to par.

INDEX